Another World

Another World

A Retreat in the Ozarks

William Claassen

SHEED & WARD
Lanham • Chicago • New York • Toronto • Plymouth, UK

Excerpt on p. vi from *Wisdom Distilled from the Daily: Living the Rule of St. Benedict Today* by Joan Chittister. Copyright © 1990 by Joan Chittister. Reprinted by permission of HarperCollins Publishers

Published by Sheed & Ward
An imprint of Rowman & Littlefield Publishers, Inc.
4501 Forbes Boulevard, Suite 200
Lanham, MD 20706

Estover Road
Plymouth PL6 7PY
United Kingdom

Distributed by National Book Network

Copyright © 2007 by Rowman & Littlefield Publishers, Inc.

British Library Cataloguing in Publication Information Available

Library of Congress Cataloging-in-Publication Data

Claassen, William, 1948–
    Another world : a retreat in the Ozarks / William Claassen.
      p. cm.
    Includes bibliographical references.
    ISBN-13: 978-1-58051-222-0 (pbk. : alk. paper)
    ISBN-10: 1-58051-222-4 (pbk. : alk. paper)
    1. Monastic and religious life. 2. Assumption Abbey (Ava, Mo.)
  3. Claassen, William, 1948– I. Title.

BX2435.C53 2007
271'.1250778832—dc22   2007019270

Printed in the United States of America

♾™ The paper used in this publication meets the minimum requirements of American National Standard for Information Sciences—Permanence of Paper for Printed Library Materials, ANSI/NISO Z39.48-1992.

For the late Penny Lernoux,
compassionate, inspirational, and intrepid journalist

Monasteries hardly seem like places from which to analyze the world. To go to the monastery, popular mythology has it, is to leave the world, not to get even more deeply involved with it. But it may be only from a distance that we see best. It may be those who do not have money who best know that money is not essential to the good life. It may be those who each have only a bed and books and one closet full of clothes in one small room to call their own who clearly realize what clutter can do to a life. It may be those who vow obedience to another who can sense what self-centeredness can do to corrode a heart. It may be only those who stand alone in life who can really know what community is all about. It may be those who are powerless by choice who can best demonstrate the power that comes from not having power. It may be those who have decided against amassing personal property who can realize that bankruptcy and welfare and sufficiency are not the worst things that can happen to a person in life. It may be those who are unmarried by choice who can sensitively hear the abandoned and the widowed and the lonely. It may only be those who have no corporate or ecclesial ladder to climb who can best speak to equality. Indeed, the monastery gives a privileged perspective from which to speak to the world.

Joan Chittister, OSB
Wisdom Distilled from the Daily:
Living the Rule of St. Benedict Today

Contents

~

List of Illustrations*

*All illustrations are from the author's collection.

~

Acknowledgments

This book was realized with the assistance and cooperation of many people. I wish to take this opportunity to thank them.

First, I want to express my gratitude to the Trappist monks at Assumption Abbey, who have frequently welcomed me on retreat. In particular, I would like to thank Father Cyprian, Father Robert, Brother Boniface, the late Father Theodore, Father Richard, Brother Dominic, and Father Mark.

Next, I wish to thank the retreat guests who were at the abbey during my extended stay. I thoroughly enjoyed their camaraderie and greatly appreciated our conversations, particularly those in which I had the opportunity to hear someone's personal story and to share my own.

Thank you to Neil Virtue for his constructive feedback, design suggestions, and timely technical assistance. His support and patience were greatly appreciated.

And finally, I wish to thank Sara Davis, John Loudon, Sarah Stanton, Elaine McGarraugh, and Catherine Bielitz for their insights, suggestions, and revisions. Their thorough review of my manuscript was invaluable.

Introduction

I began my spiritual journey in a small town on the Kansas plains. It had once been a Santa Fe Railroad center, where cowboys drove their cattle for transport to the Chicago market and drank into the late night hours at the noisy saloons found on every block. But by the time I arrived, the town had become a church seeker's paradise. There were Presbyterians, Methodists, and Episcopalians—Mennonites, Lutherans, and Catholics—Nazarenes, Baptists, and Congregationalists—Christian Scientists, Jehovah's Witnesses, and Pentacostalists. There was even an Amish community nearby.

I recall that the Amish farmers were revered as good stewards of the land. Their organic farming practices, rooted in biblical teachings, were admired and respected.

Many church denominations were divided. And in a number of cases, they were theologically split into separate congregations. Some of the churches believed in pacifism, while others beat their war drums. There were congregations who practiced simple lifestyles and others that set no limits. There were fundamentalist preachers and there were pastors who would never have considered interpreting the Bible literally. While many churches taught evolution, some preached creationism. Although most of the faith communities worshipped reservedly, there were a few congregations who clapped their hands, stomped their feet, and spoke out loud during their celebration services.

In my hometown there were African American, Caucasian, and Hispanic houses of worship, but only a few that mixed the races. "Most folks just seem to like to worship with their own kind," I heard growing up. And over the years, that is what I have observed.

Although I was initially baptized and confirmed into the First Presbyterian Church, most of my father's kin were practicing Mennonites. Holidays and religious celebrations were influenced by both faiths. As a child, I attended Mennonite Bible School in the summer, Baptist Bible School during the academic year, and Sunday Bible School with the Presbyterians.

I grew up with the understanding that Christianity and the church stood for compassion and equality, human rights, and reconciliation, not to mention social justice. And when they didn't, something was sorely wrong.

Relatives on both sides of my family were my early role models offering examples of how to integrate faith and lifestyle. My cousins, who declared conscientious objector status and served their country through alternative service, garnered my respect. I greatly admired an aunt and uncle, who uprooted their lives and moved to the Deep South to work for the civil rights movement. And I honored the efforts of my mother's sister, who struggled to make integration a reality in the public school system where her children attended classes.

In my early teens, I had the opportunity to broaden my faith experience when I participated in a Presbyterian summer work camp on a Navajo reservation in New Mexico. There I was introduced to the Native American Church, which fused Navajo spiritual practices and Christian rituals. I discovered that the

Navajos had preserved much of their native culture by couching it in Christian terminology—a survival tactic long used by indigenous cultures in coping with their Christian conquerors.

As a high school student, I further expanded my spiritual background working for a Quaker service project in the Northeast. My fellow volunteers, committed Quakers, hailed from a dozen states. Many of them had already participated in peace demonstrations with their parents. Some had even spent a night in jail for nonviolent civil disobedience. Others had worked in soup kitchens or organized environmental projects in their hometowns.

We gathered each Sunday in the parlor of an old farmhouse for an hour of silent worship, interrupted only when one of us was moved by the Spirit to get up and speak. My workmates were teenagers whose understanding of domestic and foreign policies and world politics, not to mention biblical teachings, were far beyond my awareness. I struggled to catch up.

Over the years, my spiritual journey and work life have frequently intertwined both in the United States and abroad. I will touch on many of those varied experiences in the text. But it was in Kentucky, where I worked as a VISTA (Volunteers in Service to America) volunteer in the late 1960s, that I first became aware of monastic life.

One weekend, friends invited me to join them for a picnic near Kentucky's Abbey of Gethsemani, Thomas Merton's one-time home. I remember that they talked at length about his writings and recommended that I read his autobiography, *The Seven Storey Mountain*, which I did. But it would be another two years before I would schedule my first monastic retreat back in the Bluegrass State.

In late December 1973, I returned to Kentucky. Months earlier, I had applied for and received permission from the guest master to make a retreat at Gethsemani over the Christmas holiday. Inside Louisville's crowded and noisy bus depot, I waited anxiously for my ride. Hours later, I sat between two Trappist monks in the cab of an old Ford pickup headed for the abbey. My new acquaintances soon put me at ease. There was good conversation and laughter shared during that bumpy truck ride. The heater didn't work properly, and the heavy snowfall from the night before crunched under the tires as we drove over the country roads to the abbey.

Since that visit, I have made many retreats in various monastic settings. I have had meaningful experiences with the Benedictines at Weston Priory in Vermont, where the day begins with a sitting meditation on the floor and where liturgical dance is a common form of worship in the spring and summer months. Outside Yarmouth, Nova Scotia, I spent an Easter holiday in the coed Christian monastic community of Nova Nada. The monastery, a former hunting lodge, provided one-room hermitages, originally hunters' cabins, for every community member and each visitor.

At the end of Valle de Elqui, in a barren and mountainous region of northern Chile, I found a spiritual refuge with monks who integrated Hindu and Christian religious traditions and rituals. Inside a yurt, we observed daily prayer services sitting in a circle burning incense and ghee during purification ceremonies. It was my introduction to nontraditional monastic practices.

And I have had the good fortune to stay at Trappist monasteries situated in Oregon's forests, in rural Massachusetts, and near Virginia's Shenandoah River, just to mention a few. These monasteries continue to maintain a tradition of hospitality to the seeker.

At one time, I arranged an extended retreat at Assumption Abbey, a Trappist monastery nestled in the Ozark foothills. It was during that visit that I became keenly aware that the monastery was a community not only of monks but of visitors as well. All of us were pursuing our spiritual journey. The monks had made a commitment to live by St. Benedict's *The Rule* for the remainder of their lives. And the visitors had made a commitment to honor, respect, and oftentimes participate in the monks' way of life during their individual retreats. This book is about that Assumption Abbey experience.

I traveled to the abbey with few provisions: a tape recorder and some blank journals, a camera, two books of poetry, a songbook, and a few changes of clothes. During my stay I had the opportunity to participate in the daily rhythm of the liturgical hours, talk at length with the monks and the guests, listen to my own inner dialogue, and make personal discoveries.

My hope is to offer the reader insights into a Christian monastic community from the perspectives of the monks, the visitors, and the author. I have tried to record my retreat faithfully. Portions of many interviews are included in the book. The quotations are drawn from extensive notes, background reading, tape recordings, and memory. They reproduce as accurately as possible the statements of my hosts and my fellow guests. Names of some individuals have been changed out of respect for their privacy. In one chapter, I have combined the events of two days into one. In another chapter, I have integrated two scenes into one for the sake of clarity. When writing about a particular dream sequence, I took the liberty of expanding the dialogue to express for the reader what I already knew.

Each of the chapters represents one retreat day at the abbey. The reflections are taken from recorded conversations that I scheduled with five of the monks. And the epilogue is an account of my two-day stay at New Melleray Abbey in Iowa, the motherhouse of Assumption Abbey. I had not originally planned to stay in the Iowa community; however, after my Missouri retreat, I realized the importance of such a visit. Most of the Missouri monks had begun monastic life there.

Finally, I have included the lyrics from gospel songs and traditional spirituals after each chapter. I selected them for their relationship to what evolved for me in a spiritual and emotional way from day to day. Many are familiar old songs, and I hope that each one will convey a mood, a state of mind, and a melody. It is my way of bringing a musical rhythm to the text. Like Gregorian chants, the emotional and spirit-filled gospel songs can quickly bring me back into my relationship with creation.

Trappist Abbeys in the United States

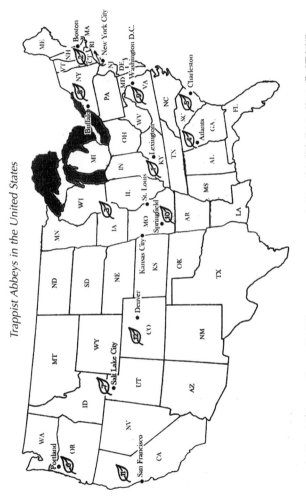

1. Abbey of Gethsemani, Trappist, KY 40051
2. St. Joseph's Abbey, Spencer, MA 01562
3. New Melleray Abbey, Peosta, IA 52068
4. Monastery of the Holy Spirit, Conyers, GA 30094
5. Mepkin Abbey, Moncks Corner, SC 29461
6. Abbey of Our Lady of Guadalupe, Lafayette, OR 97127

7. Abbey of the Holy Trinity, Huntsville, UT 84317
8. Abbey of the Genesee, Piffard, NY 14533
9. Holy Cross Abbey, Berryville, VA 22611
10. Assumption Abbey, Ava, MO 65608
11. New Clairvaux Abbey, Vina, CA 96092
12. St. Benedict's Monastery, Snowmass, CO 81654

Assumption Abbey's Daily Schedule

Weekdays

3:30 a.m.	Vigils
6:30	Lauds and Mass
7:45	Breakfast
11:45	Sext
12:00 p.m.	Lunch
5:45	Vespers
6:30	Dinner
7:40	Compline

Sundays and holidays

7:30 a.m.	Breakfast
9:00	Community Mass

CHAPTER ONE

~

Visitors Welcome

As soon as you stop the train,
you can see what cargo you are carrying.

Sister Sylvia
Stillpoint House of Prayer

I went to the woods because I wished to live deliberately,
to front only the essential facts of life, and to see if I could
not learn what it had to teach, and not, when I came to
die, discover that I had not lived.

Henry David Thoreau
Walden

"Pentecostal Holiness Temple," written in bold, uniform black
letters, jumps out from the square weathered sign planted in
the rocky soil beside the highway. Behind it stands an imposing white cross. I step on the brakes, pull off the road into a
wide gravel parking lot, stop the car, and turn off the engine.
Over the past two years, I've driven by this local house of worship a half-dozen times, nagged by an itchy sense of curiosity.

It's one of the many nondenominational churches that I pass by on this journey. Churches with names like True Light, All Nations, and Peter's Rock heavily populate this southern Missouri landscape. This one in particular draws my attention.

Once I'm out of the car, I begin to walk the property. An old, faded red Chevy pickup parked nearby is a hopeful sign. Maybe the pastor is at home. I want to inquire about his congregation.

Nestled in a clearing and surrounded by low brush and leafless trees sits a humble-looking one-story wood-frame building sorely in need of a fresh coat of white paint. Rows of brown and black shingles, a few missing here and there, layer the low-slung roof. The smell of the wet leaves that lie thick on the earth around the church permeates the cool air. Closed window blinds and a locked front door prevent me from satisfying my curiosity.

Rusty flagpoles, flying symbolic banners of religious affiliation and national identification, are planted on either side of the temple. A billowing Christian flag, red Latin cross on blue canton against a white background, claims one side. It is similar to the flag carried by the ill-fated Christian crusaders of the eleventh and twelfth centuries. On the other side hangs a frayed Old Glory. It somehow seems inappropriate and contrary to one of our country's founding principles: separation of church and state.

"Why is there an American flag hanging in the front of the sanctuary?" I remember asking a church elder when I was young. After all, I knew that Christianity's roots were in the Middle East and that the faith was practiced all over the world. Christianity didn't belong to America. "Because that's the way it ought to be," he replied.

Off to one side of the property sits a medium-size mobile home. Two wide green stripes, midway across the otherwise beige metal siding, provide its most distinguishing characteristic. There are patches of rust on the siding, and the metal skirt around the bottom could use some adjustment. I rap several times on the screen door, but there is no response.

As I shuffle through the wet leaves on my way back to the car, I think of the first time I participated in a nondenominational service. The experience was a revelation. It was during a particularly exhilarating period in my life, one full of new discoveries.

In the late 1960s, I was living in Louisville, Kentucky, and working as a VISTA volunteer in the city's West End. VISTA was the domestic Peace Corps in President Lyndon Johnson's War on Poverty.

I had joined the program after my sophomore year at a state university in the Midwest. A line from William Saroyan's much-lauded Depression-era play, titled *The Time of Your Life*, best describes that university experience—"dull, dead, boring, empty, and murderous" (p. 75). I was suffocating, and I had to break free. VISTA was the answer. After completing the training, I felt like a phoenix rising from the ashes. My work as a community organizer in the streets and the city housing projects transformed my worldview. I was privileged to work with former coal miners who were fighting for their health benefits and with empowered welfare mothers organizing to improve their daily lives. And I received tremendous support from community lawyers who had ethical standards, clergy who practiced what they preached, and scores of political activists with visions for a better world.

In my work, I was introduced to our country's labor and progressive political history, the history that had been omitted from my high school and college textbooks. I began to read about the lives of such important figures as labor organizer Elizabeth Gurley Flynn, Underground Railroad founder Sojourner Truth, Democratic Socialists Eugene Debs and Norman

Thomas, Renaissance man Paul Robeson, and anarchist Emma Goldman. "If I can't dance, I don't want to be part of your revolution!" Goldman is rumored to have proclaimed. I hadn't heard anything that lively in a classroom.

During that time, I became acquainted with progressive historical and political analysts, including Howard Zinn and Noam Chomsky. And I learned community organizing techniques by studying the work of two of the most compassionate organizers in our country: Saul Alinsky and César Chávez.

I began to pay attention to the lyrics of folk singer activists Woody Guthrie and Pete Seeger, Odetta, and Barbara Dane. Guthrie's "This Land Is Your Land" became my national anthem. And it still is.

Protestant leader William Sloane Coffin Jr., activist Catholic priests Philip and Dan Berrigan, civil rights icons Martin Luther King Jr. and Bayard Rustin, and scores of lay activists were among the many who made me sit up and take notice. They actually practiced the teachings of the biblical scriptures I had learned as a child. Those men and women opened my eyes to a Christian theology that was liberating.

Inspired by them, I began to participate in acts of nonviolent civil disobedience. It became clear to me that when my government initiated and supported repressive policies, both here and abroad, it was my patriotic duty to stand in its way and help expose the corruption. "Dissent is the highest form of patriotism," said Thomas Jefferson. My political education mushroomed when I volunteered at an antiwar coffeehouse near Fort Knox army base. On the weekends, I helped distribute its weekly alternative newspaper to enlisted men and women taking R&R in the city.

One Saturday night as I was passing out newspapers, I happened to run into my neighbor. A policeman six days a week but a preacher on Sundays, he invited me to attend the next morning's service at his storefront church. I accepted his invitation. Back then, "Holy Rollers" was the common name for his congregation and a description of their religious practices.

My upbringing, in a caring and supportive small-town Presbyterian church in south-central Kansas, hadn't prepared me for the experience on that day. A baby's cry was the most expressive emotional outburst I ever remember hearing during one of those Presbyterian services. That Sunday morning in Louisville, I spent more time standing and clapping, singing and shouting "Hallelujah" and "Amen" than I did sitting in the pew. But when the preacher invited individuals to come down front and "speak to Jesus," my Presbyterian upbringing kicked in and I held back.

However, without missing a beat, a big, handsome, proud-looking woman yelled, "Amen, I'm comin'!" and she proceeded to march down the aisle. Each heavy step of the way was a confirmation of her determination. Once near the pulpit, she began to whisper, then to talk, and finally to shout out her confession to Jesus. The woman startled me when she began to sway and sweat and dance and jump as if she were trying to shake off the devil.

I quickly joined a group of church members who moved down to the front and formed a support circle around her in case she passed out, which she did briefly. But then she came to, got herself back up, and finished what she'd set out to accomplish. "Amen!" By the time she calmed down, I was the one sweating and swaying and feeling gratefully exhausted. At the end of the service, I hugged that radiant woman hard and thanked her more times than I can remember. She reawakened something in me that had long been dormant.

At that Holy Roller celebration, it became clear to me that I—and no one else—was responsible for creating my own spiritual journey. Now, that was the gift of a lifetime. Hallelujah!

It is late afternoon. Back in the car, I start up the engine and pull onto the road, driving south with my windows down. The February weather is clear and unseasonably mild. A short time later, I spot the sign for County Road N just up ahead.

If I continued south for another hour, I could reach Branson, Missouri, the *other* country music capital of the world. Its population of five thousand welcomes more than six million visitors a year. Tonight I could have the pleasure of square dancing to the sounds of the Sho'Nuff Country Band at the Dogwood Theater or singing along with the Grand Old Gospel Players at the Dixie Stampede or maybe clapping to the tunes of Ronnie Prophet at the Indoor Pickin' Parlor.

"A lot of people go to southern Missouri to visit the number one vacation spot in the country," proclaimed Rocket, a rock 'n' roll musician and friend of mine. "And a few people venture down that way to rediscover the value of silence at a monastery." When he asked me if I knew the difference between the two choices, I said no. "Well, at the one you come back with souvenirs," said Rocket, "and at the other, you return with a different perspective."

This trip, I'm going to forgo the souvenirs and opt for the silence and the different perspective. At the county road sign, I flip on the turn signal and pull off onto a narrow two-lane road that climbs into the Ozark foothills. The blacktop curls and dips and swerves, weaving its way through the brown and gray rural terrain. Occasionally I drive past a house surrounded by a picket fence, or a mobile home partially hidden by the oncoming darkness. The drive feels longer than usual. I've been told that Assumption Abbey is the most remote Trappist monastery in the United States.

Finally, my headlights fall on a small, simple marker with an arrow and the printed word *Monastery*. I turn in and drive a few miles down the narrow, one-lane road to the wooden sign at Assumption Abbey's entrance. The long driveway winds

Abbey entrance

through a tunnel of tall trees that, in warmer weather, would create a green canopy high above me. By the time I park in the guest area, it is dark, but I can see lights through the windows of the guest quarters. I'm glad to be back.

This will be my fourth self-guided retreat at the abbey in the past few years. One of those stays was during the Christmas holiday, and another took place over an Easter weekend. However, for this spring retreat, the community has given me permission to stay longer than a week in order to become better acquainted with the monks' way of life.

I let myself in through the guest entrance and encounter Father Theodore, the community's business manager. Balding, gray-bearded, and dressed in jeans and a work shirt, he looks excited. "Welcome back," he says, peering at me over the top of his thick, black-framed glasses. I automatically sign the guest book that sits on a podium near the entrance. A community photograph hangs directly above. With fewer than twenty monks, Assumption Abbey is the smallest of the dozen Trappist monasteries in the country. Artificial wood paneling covers the walls of the visitors' parlor, which is filled with an assortment of overstuffed chairs and sofas. A few table lamps spread a welcome, warm glow around the room. The windowsills on one side of the room house a curious collection of rocks, snail shells, fossils, and small pieces of wood, added to by visitors over the years and left for the pleasure of others. I too have contributed a few of nature's souvenirs to the collection on my previous stays.

"Have you had something to eat?" inquires the monk as he leads me into the simply furnished guest dining room, which is filled with the aroma of Italian cooking. I tell him that I ate earlier.

Potted ferns and climbing vines cluster around the windows that look out into the backyard and the woods beyond. Behind us stand two extended folding tables stacked with a mismatched collection of plates, cups, and saucers. A big bowl of apples and oranges sits next to the half-filled coffeepot, as does an assortment of teas and some hot chocolate mix. I'm pleased to spot the hefty jar of crunchy peanut butter and the plastic honey bear next to the silverware tray. It's not unusual for me to come out here at all hours of the day or night, to make a peanut-butter-and-honey sandwich and a cup of hot tea.

Tables extending down the center of the room are covered with an assortment of colorful, floral-print plastic table-cloths. One of them reminds me of the cloth that covered my great-aunt Helen's kitchen table, from which she served her prized chocolate chip cookies and award-winning coconut cream pie.

Flashbacks often occur when I am on monastic retreats. I'm sometimes visited by deceased relatives, past friends, and former lovers. Significant life decisions bubble up in my memory. As Kathleen Norris writes about her retreat experience in *The Cloister Walk*, "And I have found that monasteries have a way of bringing me back to myself" (p. 305).

Paneling also overlays the walls of the refectory. This abbey was constructed in the 1950s, at a time when interiors were covered indiscriminately with inexpensive, artificial wood paneling. It was intended to create a sense of comfort and warmth, but it darkens the room and makes the space appear smaller than it is.

At one end of the dining room sits a record player from the same time period. A stack of 33 rpm albums, offering guests a musical selection ranging from Beethoven and Tchaikovsky to the Mormon Tabernacle Choir, leans precariously nearby. Above the player hangs a popular framed print of the Last Supper. It's a duplicate of the one that hung in the hallway of the First Baptist Church where I attended weekly Bible school until I was twelve years old.

"What's cooking?" I ask.

"We're having a pizza party," the monk gleefully proclaims. "I still have some special decorations to hang up before the party begins."

Father Theodore explains that the abbot from New Melleray Abbey is visiting. Located near Dubuque, Iowa, this Trappist monastery is the motherhouse, the founding community of Assumption Abbey. The abbot is accompanied by the Trappistine abbotess from Iowa's Our Lady of the Mississippi Abbey, a community of women within the same Roman Catholic order of monks (brothers) and nuns (sisters). They make an annual visit here to inquire about the well-being of the community, a common practice of Trappist monasteries. "They are here to assist, not judge," Theodore tells me. "Tomorrow they will be returning to their respective communities." But before they leave, they will share their observations and recommendations.

I offer to help him with the decorations, but he says that won't be necessary. He leads me down the dimly lit, gray-tiled hallway to my room in the visitors' wing. Taped to the door is a manila card on which my name has been printed. "As you know, the final service of the day will be at 7:40, if you would like to join us," he says. He exits quietly, closing the door behind him.

A dark-orange throw rug next to the twin bed adds color and warmth to the beige tiles and pale green walls. Over the bed hangs a small black cross. The room is familiar; I stayed here on my first Assumption Abbey retreat. Next to the curtained window sits a three-drawer wooden desk and one of those nondescript overstuffed chairs. Fresh linens hang by the corner sink next to the door leading into the bathroom. The pleasant smell of Ivory soap fills the room.

On the desk next to the lamp sits a worn Jerusalem Bible and a daily schedule for meals and liturgical services, commonly known as the Divine Office. There are five services in the sanctuary throughout the day, beginning with Vigils at 3:30 a.m. and ending with Compline at 7:40 p.m.

This rigorous routine, established in the eleventh century by the Roman Catholic Cistercian Order of Monks in Cîteaux, France, maintains a daily discipline of prayer, study, and manual labor. The Trappists acquired their name six hundred years later, during a reform movement at the Cistercian Abbey of La Trappe. The reformers advocated a more austere way of life, a return to the original teachings of St. Benedict.

Rather than unpack, I undress and take a shower. Standing under the soothing hot water, I review images of the day, which flicker past my mind's eye. Stepping out of the shower, I dry off and pull on a pair of faded blue jeans and an old green plaid flannel shirt with a hole in the left elbow. It's a favorite of mine.

From my book bag, I remove a black vinyl-covered journal, a tape recorder, blank tapes, and a copy of St. Benedict's *The Rule*—the primary authority on the nuts and bolts of Roman Catholic monastic life. The last three items out of the bag are *The Rag and Bone Shop of the Heart: Poems for Men*, the joyful *Rise Up Singing: The Group Singing Songbook*, and a copy of *Life Prayers from Around the World: 365 Prayers, Blessings, and Affirmations to Celebrate the Human Journey*.

After hanging up my clothes and camera bag and putting away my shaving gear, I sit down at the desk. Turning on the lamp, I slowly open and close the new-smelling journal a few times to loosen up the binding, and begin to write. It's not long before the medieval liturgical schedule becomes a reality. A bell atop Assumption Abbey rings out across the Ozark darkness announcing Compline. The bell's toll is the keeper of time and the daily rhythm of life here.

Alone, I proceed down the hallway and past the dining room. I have an urge to stick my head in the door but decide to keep walking. "Did you hear that the president's nomination was shot down?" asks an anonymous male voice coming from the party. "Oh, no, not again," replies a woman. "I thought he was an excellent choice."

No one else is in the candlelit sanctuary as I enter and sit down in the front pew, my eyes adjusting to the soft darkness. The sanctuary, with a high ceiling and a half-dozen elongated stained-glass windows, is divided by a simple railing. On one side, the monks' podiums face the altar in a semicircle. My side is filled with wooden pews for the visitors.

There are no figures depicted in the stained glass. Instead, the windows are a collection of geometric shapes in deep reds, indigo blues, warm yellows, brilliant oranges, and forest greens that enhance the contemplative mood of the space.

In *Open to the Spirit*, Dewey Weiss Kramer writes that, historically speaking, simplicity was the key to Cistercian monastic architecture and design, especially in the sanctuary. "The architecture was to be clean, stripped of unnecessary distractions, including figurative glass." Imagery was deemed frivolous and counterproductive in monastic spirituality, according to Kramer. "One of the main functions of Cistercian art and architecture has been to discourage emotional, irrational reactions and to encourage a sense of composure, a necessary predisposition to contemplative prayer" (pp. 41, 42).

Two candles flicker at the front of the sanctuary, and the air is sweet with the smell of incense. A single icon of Mary holding the Christ child hangs directly behind the altar. Built into the wall near the icon is the tabernacle, a thick varnished cedar box with a latched door. Inside is the consecrated host, symbol of Christ's body, distributed daily during early-morning Eucharist.

On the far end of the monks' podiums is the abbot's chair and his prominent wooden staff with an encircled cross at its top. "That's called a crozier," a monk had explained during one of my past retreats. "It's like a shepherd's staff. That's the symbol, you see. An abbot is the shepherd, and we are his flock." The abbot is the symbolic Christ figure in the monastery.

I close my eyes, take a few deep breaths, and sink deeper into the wooden pew. As I open my eyes, the monks begin to enter the sanctuary through the doors leading from the cloistered living quarters of the monastery. Each monk is dressed in the traditional white habit and black scapular cinched together at the waist by a wide, thick leather belt. Following a nine-hundred-year-old tradition, the monks begin to sing and chant praises to God.

Each of the liturgical services of the Divine Office is composed of hymn singing, chanting, prayer, and scripture readings from the Book of Psalms. All 150 psalms, collected in a book called the Psalter, are recited within a designated period of time—one or two weeks, depending on the monastery.

"The antiphonal nature of the chanting furthers the sense of community within the group," writes Kramer. "And since this is the prayer of [Christian] monasteries worldwide and is

Latin psalter

Monks and novice

the prayer of the universal church, it unites the community to the whole praying church" (p. 30).

Rocket, my musician friend, once said, "These are the guys [gals] that are up at 3 a.m. praying and chanting and holding the universe together." If this is true, and I believe it is, then I am also most grateful to the Buddhist, Hindu, Jain, and Sufi monks around the world who are praying and chanting throughout the day and night. I am confident that they, too, hold together their share of the universe.

At the conclusion of Compline, the monks close the day by turning to Mary's icon and singing the Salve Regina, Mater Misericordiae, as monks have done for more than a millennium. "To you do we send up our sighs, mourning, and weeping in this vale of tears," they sing in unison. When the brothers line up in front of Abbot Cyprian, I follow directly behind. Each of us bows slightly before the abbot and is sprinkled with holy water. The monks leave the sanctuary, and I return to my pew in the darkness.

Each time I participate in this ritual, I feel as though I am experiencing a group baptism. Tonight, I witness more than that. With eyes closed, I visualize the stark black-and-white photograph of a Louisiana river baptism taken by Keith M. Calhoun. His camera captured two African American church elders preparing to take a candidate under the water. "A picture is like a prayer," commented photographer Harry Callahan, a Calhoun contemporary, in a *Creative Camera International Yearbook* interview (p. 76). And I revisit the memory of a baptism that I recently witnessed at a friend's Pentecostal church, where a tall, heavyset man dressed in flowing white robes was completely submerged in a water tank behind the pulpit. A few sprinkles of holy water have brought forth a flood of images.

On the way back to my room, I detour into the guest refectory and discover Father Theodore standing on tiptoe on a chair. He's taking one of four printed banners down from the wall. "I made them for the party," he explains, looking down at me with a sheepish grin on his face. "I have a new computer program that allows me to make these. So I thought I'd give it a try."

"Zacchaeus, hurry down, I mean to have a PARTY at your house!" proclaims the banner that he holds in his hands. "VIBRANT VISITATION!" shouts a second banner hanging directly across the room. We laugh as I help him remove a third one that reads, "Jesus said to the disciples, there is no need for them to disperse. Give them a PARTY yourselves!" He takes down the fourth banner by himself, a greeting that hangs from the front wall: "Welcome to Abbot Brendan and Abbotess Gale." On either side of their names are the familiar Chinese symbols of yin and yang, the signs of male and female, symbols of opposites. "I thought they were appropriate for the occasion," Theodore says as he rolls it up. Bringing the abbotess to participate in the annual review is a relatively new practice. "A female perspective is now a valued part of the review," he tells me.

A Trappist brother once commented, "Monks have one foot in the contemporary world and one foot in the ancient world of monastic life." That reality becomes clearer to me on each retreat.

After preparing a cup of tea, I bid the monastery's computer expert a good night and return to my room. Placing the teacup carefully on the desk top, I sit down and begin to leaf through my copy of St. Benedict's *The Rule*. Written in the sixth century, *The Rule* provides instructions on all facets of Roman Catholic monastic life, from electing an abbot and establishing a governing body to determining clothing allowances, diet, and specific times for prayer. It is a practical and workable manifesto that advocates "from each according to his ability and to each according to his need."

The Rule speaks to the essence of Acts 4:32: "The community of believers was of one heart and one mind. None of them ever claimed anything as his own; rather, everything was held in common." Benedict's framework has shaped cenobitic monastic life for more than a millennium.

"Listen carefully, my son, to the master's instructions, and attend to them with the ear of your heart," writes Benedict in the prologue. "This is advice from a father who loves you; welcome it, and faithfully put it into practice" (p. 1).

He suggests that the monastery is an academic institution. "Therefore we intend to establish a school for the Lord's service. In drawing up its regulations, we hope to set down nothing harsh, nothing burdensome. The good of all concerned, however, may prompt us to a little strictness in order to amend faults and to safeguard love." He instructs the abbot to "arrange everything so that the strong have something to yearn for and the weak nothing to run from" (p. 3).

After closing the book I open the window. The cold night air rushes into the small room. I spread two extra blankets over the bed, turn out the lights, and crawl between the sheets.

Amazing Grace

by John Newton

Amazing grace! How sweet the sound,
That saved a soul like me.
I once was lost and now am found,
Was blind but now I see.

'Twas grace that taught my heart to fear,
And grace my fears relieved.
How precious did that grace appear,
The hour I first believed.

Through many dangers, toils and snares,
I have already come.
'Tis grace that brought me safe thus far,
And grace will lead me home.

~

CHAPTER TWO

Trappist Geography Unfolds

The soul knows for certain
only that it is hungry.

Simone Weil
Waiting for God

Monasticism is among the oldest of human archetypes;
like the family, like marriage, like the complex rituals of
desire, it predates recorded history. It is less a manifesta-
tion of any particular religious tradition than an outgrowth of the human imperative to ask why.

Fenton Johnson
Keeping Faith

The monastery bell begins to ring, announcing Vigils and the
start of a new day. I get up without hesitation, shut the window, pull on my clothes, sit down at the desk, and begin to
write. Rather than attend the early-morning liturgy, I feel an
urgent need to record the dream from which I awakened at the
bell's ringing.

The dream is set in the old high school gymnasium where my father demonstrated his athletic prowess as a basketball star. Thirty years later, I led high school assemblies there as the student body president.

I walk out onto the varnished gym floor, and I look up into the bleachers where anonymous spectators are talking in muffled voices. Under my arm I carry an oversized special edition of Na-tional Geographic with an equally large map enclosed. The issue is dedicated to the Trappist monasteries scattered throughout the United States.

I place the magazine on the first tier of bleachers, remove the map, walk to center court, place the map on the polished wooden floor, and begin to open it up. But the more parts I unfold, the more there seem to be to unfold. I feel anxious, begin to sweat, and work faster. The coated paper is unwieldy.

"Go, Bill, go! Go, Bill, go! Go, Bill, go!" shout the spectators. I move even faster to unfold the huge map upon which each monastery location is designated by a vivid green space marked with symbols for plowed fields and woodlands. "Go, go, go, go, go, go!" The observers yell even louder and in unison—as if there are five seconds left in the game, the score is tied, and I'm standing at the free-throw line with the basketball in hand.

Finally, I successfully lay out the last quarter of the map and re-lease a triumphant holler so loud that the observers fall silent. The map covers the entire basketball court.

Over the past two decades, I have made retreats in six of these communities. Each of the monasteries, when it was es-tablished, fulfilled the requirement of the Cistercian (Trappist) constitution to be "far from the haunts of men."

Looking out over the vast green map, I decide to walk over to the Abbey of Gethsemani near Bardstown, Kentucky.

Gethsemani, founded in 1848, was the first successful Trappist monastery in the United States. The pioneer monks, originally from western France, initially lived in log cabins and farmed the land. Today, the monks draw a significant portion of their income from cheese and fruitcake businesses.

The Trappist Thomas Merton, a prolific writer on spiritual and social matters, was a Gethsemani monk. Merton's classic autobiography, *The Seven Storey Mountain,* is a vivid and detailed account of his spiritual journey. The book has influenced countless men and women seriously considering the monastic life.

It was here that I made my first retreat in December 1973. I can still visualize scenes that were an integral part of that experience. There was the Christmas Eve Mass, where mysterious events unfolded amid a haze of incense and smoke from the candles. It was my introduction to the antiphonal sounds of Gregorian chant emanating from hooded, faceless figures that appeared to float through the sanctuary. A sparsely furnished room with a cold, bare floor, firm mattress, and a crucifix hanging on the wall was where I fell asleep each night. And there were the long periods of silence throughout those winter days.

The solo walks in the dense Kentucky woods and my visits to the onetime hermitage of Thomas Merton remain in my memory. That simple, concrete-block abode was my daily pilgrimage site. Not once during my stay did I feel awkward, uncomfortable, or out of place.

I knew when I left the abbey that monastic retreats would become an important part of my life, a refuge of sorts. I had found a spiritual community that understood my hunger for periods of silence and solitude, a community that strove for cooperation rather than competition.

Looking out from Kentucky, I walk toward the northeast and stop at St. Joseph's Abbey near Spencer, Massachusetts.

Built with native stone from the area, St. Joseph's architectural design is medieval in appearance. It, too, is surrounded by acres of woods and farmland, some of which it leases to its neighbors.

My retreat at St. Joseph's, on a Thanksgiving holiday, was a solo journey. I spent most of my time meditating, taking long walks, and reading literature on comparative religions. Although I recall the sanctuary as cold and dark, the oak-paneled dining room always felt warm and inviting.

During my stay, I had hoped to meet Trappist M. Basil Pennington, another prolific writer and leading figure in the Christian meditative practice of centering prayer. His spiritual travel books on Mount Athos, Greece, and India have been particularly inspirational to me. Unfortunately, he was away from the monastery facilitating a workshop on centering prayer, for which he had received permission from his abbot.

I vividly remember a stimulating conversation with an African American monk who was also a weight lifter. He was planning to leave the United States soon and relocate to a Trappist monastery in East Africa. I was pleased to share with him my experiences in the Peace Corps in Kenya, just a few years before.

Next, I move down the eastern coastline and plant my feet in Virginia at the Holy Cross Abbey. Located near the Shenandoah River, it was built on the site of a Civil War battle.

During the time that I lived in nearby Washington, D.C., and worked with Latin American immigrants, I experienced a difficult period in my personal life when high anxiety was a constant companion. That's what prompted my midweek retreat to Holy Cross.

The abbey provided precisely what I needed—a quiet and supportive community in which to confront my issues. Helpful conversations with a brother, meditation in the chapel, and long walks in the surrounding countryside proved to be important healing activities.

Leaving Virginia, I take giant steps diagonally across the lush, green-colored map until I reach Our Lady of the Holy Spirit near Atlanta, Georgia.

I celebrated Christmas here. Author William Least Heat-Moon's experiences at Holy Spirit, recorded in *Blue Highways: A Journey into America,* encouraged my visit.

According to monastic lore, the first Georgia monks had to share a converted barn with their livestock and farm equipment until they were able to build a pine-board monastery. Now they have separate bedrooms and make stained-glass windows, prune bonsai trees, and grow produce to keep their community solvent.

After attending Christmas Mass at Holy Spirit, I was invited to a joyful celebration in the undercroft of the church. The monks and scores of locals celebrated the holiday as one large extended family. It was clear that the monastery was an important member of the wider community.

My final trek on the National Geographic *map takes me up into the Northwest and the state of Oregon.*

While residing in Portland, I arranged a lengthy visit at the Our Lady of Guadalupe Abbey, a hilltop community at the end of a long driveway that winds its way through hundreds of acres of farmland.

It was one of the few times that I made a retreat with a friend. We both worked for the public defender's office, and we belonged to the same inner-city Catholic parish. The retreat gave us the opportunity to decompress and reconnect with our souls. Beyond meditation and services, I remember being encouraged by one of the monks, a long-distance runner, to take a few invigorating runs in the rain, which I did.

But it was our departure that left a lasting impression. Unfortunately, I had become so introspective and relaxed during the visit that when I drove out onto the highway to return home, I failed to look both ways and sideswiped an oncoming car. Although there was considerable damage to both automobiles, luckily there were no physical injuries.

Finished with my tour, I return to center court, look up into the bleachers and make a request: "Will some of you folks help me fold up this map?"

"Sure," a few people yell back, and unfamiliar individuals descend the bleachers onto the floor. As we fold it up, a bell begins to ring.

It is Assumption Abbey's bell, waking me. By 4 a.m., I complete the last journal entry and close the book. I walk barefoot from the room, go quietly down the dark hallway, and turn into the refectory. After preparing a cup of hot chocolate, I sit contentedly in the dark and stare out the windows.

The southern Missouri sky is clear and sprinkled with stars. A full moon reveals the outline of the trees and shrubs out away from the monastery. Not far behind them are limestone bluffs that plunge down to a clear stream.

"Shhhhhh," I caution myself. Something is coming out of the trees. Two deer and a fawn gracefully emerge from the darkness and cautiously move toward the abbey. I hold still. The deer approach a few steps more and stop abruptly. They sense my presence. The threesome whirls around and retreats swiftly into the safety of the evergreen camouflage. Their brief appearance is nature's gift. I finish my hot chocolate and return to bed.

I reawaken with the bell announcing Lauds, but I am held fast by the layers of blankets covering me and hover in that state of consciousness midway between wakefulness and slumber. It always takes time to adjust to the daily rhythm of monastic life. For the first few days, I go to bed earlier and get up later than usual.

"The thing that everybody has to remember is that the monastery is a place where withdrawal is honored and respected and, most of all, preserved," comments a Trappist abbot in Frank Bianco's *Voices of Silence: Lives of the Trappists Today*. "But it's a notion of withdrawal, not desertion" (p. 203).

At breakfast I serve myself a bowl of oatmeal, a glass of orange juice, and a slice of whole wheat toast, then join two other guests at a table.

The man on my right, John, is tall and thin with white hair. He speaks with a slow, easy Southern drawl and wears casual slacks with a red pullover sweater. "I'm a Methodist minister," he tells me. His congregation is in rural Tennessee. Curious, I ask why he came all the way to Missouri for a retreat. "A good friend of mine, a professor at a theology school, recommended that I come here." His friend, also a Protestant clergyman, has a long and intimate relationship with the Missouri monks.

Michael, a heavyset, bearded, gregarious fellow, is the other man at our table. He measures his words in conversation and listens intently when others talk. "I'm a Glenmary priest, and I work in rural Kentucky," he tells us. His full beard, workmen's boots, and overalls give the impression of a laborer rather than a Catholic priest.

"I was a VISTA Volunteer in Kentucky for two years back in the late 1960s," I tell him. "I worked as a community organizer and received a lot of support from activist priests and Catholic nuns in Louisville."

"No kidding. I probably know some of them," replies Michael. "My parish is located in a blue-collar town in the eastern part of the state." He also mentions that he has worked in Harlan County.

"I know Harlan County," I tell him. "I worked with former miners from there who suffered from black lung." I explain that for years local doctors on the company payroll told the miners that there was no need to worry about coal dust and bad underground air. When some of the miners were diagnosed with black lung, the company denied them medical and disability benefits. The miners took them to court and successfully pressured them to provide adequate medical benefits and make significant improvements in the mines. An Academy Award–winning documentary, *Harlan County USA*, exposed the corruption there and created a broader awareness of the miners' struggle.

"My first arrest for civil disobedience was in Louisville," I comment. "The VISTA experience was a real eye-opener for me."

Michael chuckles. "I have had my share of arrests for civil disobedience, too," he admits, "but they took place in other parts of the country." Immediately, I feel a sense of camaraderie with him.

As the three of us share our personal stories, Brother Dominic sticks his round, balding head out from the kitchen. "Okay, fellows, it's time to clean up the breakfast dishes." He spots me at the table. "Hello, Claassen, I didn't know you were blessing us with another visit," he says jokingly.

Brother Dominic, the guest master's assistant, has the look and carriage of a wrestler. He walks with an easy, rolling gait, and he has a slight hunch to his broad shoulders. He is quick to make a joke.

"I came here in the mid-1980s from the monastery in California," I hear him telling John as I wipe down the table. He is referring to the Abbey of New Clairvaux near Chico. I'm surprised. I had always assumed that he was one of the pioneers at this abbey.

Finished with breakfast clean-up, I leave the monastery and walk out onto the winding driveway. The sun is out, but this morning is cooler than yesterday. I go back inside briefly to grab another sweater and my camera. Unpredictable temperatures make it wise to dress in layers during Missouri winters. "One day you're having a barbecue, and the next day you're shoveling snow" is a common saying in the Show-Me State.

Outside again, I follow the driveway for a minute and then turn off onto a familiar narrow path that cuts through the underbrush. The air is heavy with the smell of mulch. I meander and consider what images might best illustrate this monastic setting. Perhaps the bell atop the chapel or the small cemetery dotted with stark, white iron crosses. Maybe one of the signs that reads "Monastic Enclosure: Please Don't Walk Beyond This Point," or a photograph of the fruitcake assembly line in the bakery. The rum-soaked cakes have a nationwide reputation.

Upon my return to the abbey I cross paths with Father Theodore in the visitors' parlor. "If possible, I would like to change rooms, get one farther down the hallway," I tell him. "Last night my next-door neighbor had a healthy snore." Theodore reveals that he, too, heard the noise. He happened to be staying in the guest master's room last night. We laugh about the spiritual vibrations through the concrete-block walls. He is sympathetic and reassigns me to a room farther down the corridor, to which I promptly move my things.

Settled into my new living space, which is practically identical to my old room, I return to the reading of St. Benedict's manifesto. Early in his work, Benedict makes a distinction among the four types of monks.

The first are cenobites: that is, those who live in a monastery under a rule or an abbot.

Community cemetery

Assumption Abbey is a cenobitic community, as are all Trappist monasteries.

> The second kind is that of anchorites or hermits, who not in the first fervor of conversion, but after a long trial in the monastery, and already taught by the example of others, have learned to fight against the devil and are well prepared to go in faith from the brotherhood to the single combat of the desert.

To my knowledge, there are at least two men in this community who have received permission to live as hermits on the monastery grounds. I hope to meet with one of them, Father Robert, during my stay.

St. Benedict writes that the third kind of monk, the Sarabite, is "detestable."

> [They] have not been tried under any Rule nor schooled by the experienced master, as gold is tried in the furnace; [they] have a character as soft as lead.

In the very early Christian church, there were men and women who chose to live as monks without an ecclesiastical ruling or adherence to a fixed rule. They often lived in community and supported one another in their religious and spiritual practices. For whatever reasons, maybe simply their circumstances, they chose to live under their own rule.

> The fourth class of monks is called the Gyrovagi or the wanderers. [Benedict is even more critical of these spiritual seekers.] These move about all their lives through various countries, staying as guests for three or four days at different monasteries. . . . [T]hey are always on the move and never settle down, and are slaves to their own wills and to the enticement of gluttony. In every way they are worse than Sarabites.

Perhaps he was most critical of these individuals because they put a strain on the cenobitic communities and, in his eyes, fostered a negative perception of the monk's life. In closing, he clearly states a preference.

> Leaving these therefore aside, let us set down a Rule for Cenobites, who are the best kind of monk.

Midday prayer comes as a welcome respite from my time with St. Benedict. Melodious chant fills the sanctuary as I enter and take a seat behind the railing. Father Robert, the hermit monk with whom I am hoping to meet, stands among his brothers, all of them facing the altar.

Tall and lean, with short salt-and-pepper hair and a long "Father Time" beard, Robert blends in with the rest of the community as they chant the psalms. I have been told that he continues to participate in the Divine Office and community duties at designated times throughout the week. According to St. Benedict's writings, Robert is considered an anchorite, a solo monk who has "learned to fight against the devil."

Robert's physical presence brings to mind Dick, an old friend of mine who studied for the Episcopal priesthood at New York's Union Theological Seminary. The resemblance between the two men is uncanny. At the conclusion of World War II, Dick promptly volunteered to relocate to Japan to help rebuild that devastated country. He has remained there, adopting the culture as his own, making only periodic visits back to the United States.

Dick and I met when we were residents at Pendle Hill, a Quaker study and retreat center outside Philadelphia. For nine months we lived, worked, and studied in the Quaker environment. Each day began and ended with a silent Quaker meeting for worship, and our classroom work varied from spiritual writing and poetry to scriptural study and pottery making. It was a creative and contemplative daily schedule, which allowed time for internal exploration and the growth of meaningful friendships.

I was in my thirties, and Dick was in his seventies. However, age didn't make much difference. The two of us used to climb trees together on the Pendle Hill grounds. Dick, as limber as any man half his age, could usually outclimb me. He was a committed vegetarian and an advocate of "A spoonful of honey a day keeps the doctor away."

During the Pendle Hill spring semester, our community decided to observe the ancient Christian ritual of foot washing within the context of an evening religious service, as the recognition of the Divine in each of us. Dick and I were paired. I will never forget that evening celebration, when I gently washed my elder's feet. When our roles were reversed, I felt a powerful emotional reaction welling up inside my chest. It was an honor to share that experience with my friend.

"I was raised to believe that rituals were meaningless in the modern world, meant to be outgrown, like superstitions. I was educated to mistrust the rich ambiguity of symbols," recalls Kathleen Norris in *Cloister Walk* (p. 315). I, too, was raised in such an environment, but I began to claim the power and significance of symbols and rituals in my late teenage years. I longed for their meaning, their richness and power, and I sought them out whenever possible.

Years later, I had the opportunity to visit Dick in Japan. He invited me to stay in his austere living quarters, where we meditated together before his small altar, cooked simple meals over his single-burner hot plate, and slept on firm tatami mats that covered the floor.

At lunch, a fourth man joins John, Michael, and me. "My name is Matthew," he announces as he sits down at the table.

"I'm seventy-eight years old, and this is my first retreat," he declares as we eat our grilled-cheese sandwiches and tomato soup. "Maybe it will make a better man out of me."

An assembly plant retiree, Matthew looks disheveled, and he sits slightly hunched over in his chair. A gentle, friendly man, he wears a long-sleeved red-and-black checked shirt, carpenter's pants held up by suspenders, and a baseball cap. His tired-looking eyes suggest he's had a hard life. Matthew tells us that he is hearing-impaired.

"Are you staying for the week?" inquires Michael, raising his voice and looking directly at Matthew.

"Well, I don't know," replies the newcomer. "I just came here on my own accord and they put me in the visitors' cabin out a ways from the monastery." Matthew slowly pulls a light blue handkerchief from his back pocket, blows his nose, folds the handkerchief with care, and sticks it back into his pocket. "It's okay, though. I'm used to not having all the conveniences." Without much of a pause, he continues, "I had triple-bypass surgery two years ago." Maybe that's why he's on retreat, I speculate, as I consider the cautious expression in his deep-set brown eyes. This retreat is a time to think things through.

For a split second I clearly see my grandfather superimposed over the figure of Matthew, but the image quickly fades. My grandfather, dead for more than a quarter of a century, is my namesake and an infrequent visitor on my retreats. I'm surprised. He usually makes an appearance in my dreams rather than during daylight hours.

When Matthew discovers that all three of us have lived in either Tennessee or Kentucky, he begins to tell of his travels in that part of the country. Pausing only to refill our coffee cups, we stay at the table, swapping stories and talking as if we had common roots.

"Tell us about the Glenmary order," I say, looking over at Michael.

"Well, it was established in the late 1930s for the purpose of providing priests to rural areas in the South." He says that the order is primarily in the Southeast, where the Roman Catholic Church hasn't traditionally had a lot of influence. "Most of my parishioners are factory workers."

When the conversation hits a lull, I excuse myself and clear my dishes. Each guest is responsible for cleaning up after himself. I wash, dry, and put the place setting away, and exit through the guest entrance.

Outside, images of my grandfather reemerge, and childhood memories with him flash by: playing cards, raking leaves in the autumn, sitting together on his porch identifying star formations on a summer night. And there we are standing in silence, side by side, fishing in a muddy Kansas pond. As W. Paul Jones says in *Teaching the Dead Bird to Sing: Living the Hermit Life Without and Within*, "Feelings and thoughts and hands and sun and feet and leaves are getting childishly tangled, as I live out this new image of God taking birth inside of me" (p. 172).

My grandfather grew up a pacifist in the Mennonite Church. When he married my grandmother, a Presbyterian, he was promptly excommunicated. Their marriage was quite the small-town scandal, so I was told. I laugh aloud when I recall that my grandfather's closest and most colorful friend was the local Catholic priest. Once a week, they would meet at my grand-dad's house, drink a scotch and soda or two, and swap stories. Once in a while I had the pleasure of hearing the stories, when my grandfather would repeat them to me.

I remove my sweater and tie the sleeves around my waist as I continue to walk. It's warmer now than it was this morning. For the first time in all my visits I notice the stations of the cross, a series of small circular pieces of varnished wood that have been mounted and nailed to the trunks of a group of towering evergreens. They depict Christ's final journey through Jerusalem. Some of the scenes, finely etched into the wood, can be clearly distinguished, while dirt and moss partially cover others. I follow them one by one through the grove.

Years ago when I traveled to Israel to work in a collective agricultural community, I spent a week in Jerusalem's Old City. On my second day there, I joined a group of religious pilgrims to walk the Via Dolorosa, the route that Christ is said to have followed on his way to the crucifixion. It begins where Christ appeared before Pontius Pilate and concludes at the location of his murder, now enclosed in the Church of the Holy Sepulcher. According to the biblical account of that day, there were fourteen stops along that torturous route. That experience of having followed in Christ's footsteps has brought a reality to these stations of the cross.

I continue on to the other side of the gravel driveway and hike down the path as it descends toward one of the clear streams that meander through the wooded property. At the bottom and farther along on the path, limestone bluffs soar upward on either side of the trail.

The sun's warmth sends shivers up my spine and makes me drowsy. Just off the path, amidst the dead leaves, is a fallen tree trunk stripped of its bark. I untie my sweater and peel off my shirts, spread them out on the trunk, lie down, and taste the afternoon. My bare chest absorbs the sun's rays, and my eyelids drift closed—but not for long.

Crows, circling directly above me, begin to caw madly. Perhaps they are angry at my intrusion into their territory. I lie still in the hope that I can blend in with the surroundings, but they persist until I speak up in my defense. "I promise to leave in thirty minutes," I shout up at the threatening flutter of birds. "And I will leave everything just as I found it." They quiet down and leave me to rest.

Do monks ever have the time to strip down to their waists and soak up the sun's rays? I wonder. In a small community like Assumption Abbey, I would guess that the schedule can become so demanding that there is little time for recreation.

"Cenobite monks are to be occupied in manual labor, reading and, and above all, in the liturgy of the church," writes St. Benedict in *The Rule*. "The former includes not merely labor in the fields, but the exercise of any art in which some might be proficient, the result of which might be sold for the benefit of the monastery, or be in any other way useful for the good" (p. 45).

I sit up suddenly. Someone is walking nearby; the leaves crackle underneath his shoes. A monk passes by at a brisk pace, never looking in my direction. Instead of following the path, he creates his own route and playfully meanders in and out of the leaves, limbs, and fallen tree trunks as if he's maneuvering through an obstacle course. His worn blue jeans, heavy navy blue sweater, and stocking cap give him the look of a dockworker as he kicks up the leaves with glee. His obvious pleasure shatters the stereotypical image of the solemn Christian monk.

For a quarter of a century, I have been privileged to participate in contemplative retreats in Benedictine, Carmelite, and Trappist monasteries in North and South America. I have made these spiritual journeys as a Protestant, as a confirmed Roman Catholic, and later, as a committed attendee of Quaker meeting for worship. In most cases my journeys have been solo and self-guided. And I have always felt welcomed by the monks.

"What I find most appealing is their coherence to words and action, altar and pulpit, being and doing, work and leisure, silence and sound, outer and inner, fast and feast, self and community, promise and foretaste, realism and hope," comments

W. Paul Jones in *Teaching the Dead Bird to Sing* (p. 13). His words speak my sentiments.

What I discover repeatedly is that these communities are inclusive and nonjudgmental. I am free to participate or not participate in their services and meet with a spiritual adviser if I so desire. The retreats are not an escape, but rather an opportunity to come face to face with my shadows and with my light.

"Our real journey in life is interior: it is a matter of growth, deepening, and of an ever-greater surrender to the creative action of love and grace in our hearts," Thomas Merton wrote in a letter included in his *Asian Journal*. "Never was it more necessary for us to respond to that action" (p. 296).

I pull on my shirts, tie the sweater around my waist again, and begin the hike back to the monastery. The woods are deliciously hazy, illuminated by the late afternoon sun. A golden veil overlays everything in sight.

Father Richard, the official guest master, looks up from a table as I enter the refectory, remove my sweater, and make a cup of tea. He wears the black-and-white Trappist uniform. "I'm finally getting my Christmas cards written two months late," he laments. "And I will welcome yet another excuse to put them on hold if you would care to talk." He puts down his pen, removes his thick glasses, and begins to rub his bloodshot eyes. He pushes his chair away from the table and motions for me to take a seat nearby. Richard is a good talker, and I always enjoy our conversations.

"Contrary to popular belief, a vow of silence was never taken by the Trappists. In the old days, you could always talk to two people: the superior [abbot] and the novice master," explains Richard, when I ask him about the practice of silence. "However, we always had complete silence from 8 p.m. until 6 a.m." In contemporary Trappist life, there is respect for silence as well as flexibility in observing it. But meals, for the monks, are eaten without conversation. And monks and guests are strongly encouraged to honor the "great silence" between 8 p.m. and 6 a.m. Silence is a discipline, like the monks' vegetarian diet. "Abstain entirely from eating the flesh of four-footed animals," commands St. Benedict (p. 34).

According to Trappist tradition, hospitality extends to people of all faiths, both Christian and non-Christian, Richard tells me. "On the average, five hundred people make a retreat here every year. Many more non-Catholics come on retreat now." Our conversation is cut short by the bell announcing Vespers.

At the evening meal, I sit with John, the Methodist minister. Michael and Matthew must have eaten earlier or decided to forgo supper. "Do you make regular retreats?" I ask, breaking our comfortable silence.

"I frequently make weekend retreats at a House of Prayer that a friend of mine sponsors," John answers. His friend, a United Methodist minister, became acquainted with the concept when he went on sabbatical from his ministry. "He took a year off, which is unusual for a United Methodist minister, and visited various retreat centers around the United States," says John between mouthfuls of soup. "He would go to a retreat center and stay there until he felt moved to travel on to the next one on his schedule." After his friend completed the sabbatical, he knew that he wanted to create a House of Prayer for others to use. "After he retired, he and his wife bought some acreage that has two cabins on it. They moved into one and set the other aside as a House of Prayer. I also go there to meet with him as my spiritual director," adds John. "He's very good."

"I didn't realize that spiritual directors existed until I became involved with a Catholic parish," I tell him. "From what I understand, most spiritual directors are formally trained and provide their services at little or no cost."

John agrees. His friend sees the role as a continuation of his ministerial calling, although he is officially retired. We fall

Abbey twilight

back into silence, clear the table, wash our dishes, and walk together to the final service of the day.

I remain in the darkened sanctuary after Compline and think
about my dinner conversation with John. What an intriguing
idea—a "House of Prayer." The concept could be slightly altered, made more inclusive, and given the name "House of Meditation." I leave the chapel excited about the possibility for such
houses of silent worship all over the country.

When I move outside for a night walk I encounter Dyers, the community dog and self-appointed abbey guard. Covered with wiry black-and-white fur, he's the size of a Brittany spaniel. Dyers sneaks up behind me and intrudes upon the quiet with an irritating bark. When I turn around to face him his bark transforms into a growl, and he bares his teeth. Dyers and I have always had a difficult relationship. We need a mediator.

Just as I'm thinking that, Father Theodore comes outside with a flashlight in hand. "He has a mind of his own, you know," says the monk, as he walks over to the dog and talks with him. "The dog is extremely protective." After their conference Dyers turns around and struts away, Theodore returns to the monastery, and I continue with my walk.

Later, back in my room, I return to *The Rule* to read what St. Benedict wrote about visitors. Dyers's reception has prompted my self-doubt. "All guests who present themselves are to be welcomed as Christ, for He himself will say: I was a stranger and you welcomed me. Proper honor must be shown to all, especially to those who share our faith and to pilgrims," he writes (p. 42). I am reassured.

Motherless Child

Sometimes I feel like a motherless child.
Sometimes I feel like a motherless child.
Sometimes I feel like a motherless child.
A long way from home.
A long way from home.

Sometimes I feel like I never been born.
Sometimes I feel like I never been born.
Sometimes I feel like I never been born.
A long way from home.
A long way from home.

Sometimes I feel like a feather in the air.
Sometimes I feel like a feather in the air.
Sometimes I feel like a feather in the air.
A long way from home.
A long way from home.

⤺ **Reflection** ⤺

[W]hen someone accepts the title of abbot, he should direct his disciples by a twofold teaching. That means he should demonstrate everything that is good and holy by his deeds more than his words.

When he must correct someone, he should act prudently and not overdo it. If he is too vigorous in removing the rust, he may break the vessel. Let him always be wary of his own brittleness, and remember not to break the bent reed.

St. Benedict
The Rule

Father Cyprian

"I don't think the most vital thing is how or why you become a monk, but the most vital thing is why you continue to be a monk," replies Abbot Cyprian when I ask about his calling. We are sitting in my room talking. "It is why I am staying, not why I came.

"Each person has a different story as to how or why they came to do God's work," Cyprian says. He pauses, looking down at his large hands, which are resting on his knees. "In my own case I was getting into a lot of turmoil, spiritual darkness, confusion, not being able to find peace in my life."

Father Cyprian explains that he felt he needed to make the greatest sacrifice possible in order to attain the gift of faith. "I figured the Trappist monastery was the end of the road. That's why I came. And it's not the healthiest or best motivation."

Curious, I ask him what he means by "the end of the road." "It was the end of anything I wanted out of life; saying goodbye to anything like values, goals, and desires. As I say, it was not the best motivation, but for me it worked."

The abbot has the rangy build and long reach of a basket-ball player. Behind the wire-rimmed glasses, his eyes give the impression that he is analyzing events in the moment. Cyprian frequently ponders my questions, and his answers are measured and thoughtful.

He joined New Melleray Abbey in 1950 without taking the time to visit other Trappist communities around the country. "A couple of my seminary classmates had joined New Melleray a year before I did. And a little Dutch priest who was one of our spiritual directors had also joined. So in a sense I tagged along after them." He was seeking the peace of mind that he hadn't found elsewhere.

Not until he had been at the monastery for five years did he begin to experience clarity of self in relationship to the world and a sense of peace. "It was partly discipline, under-standing, and spiritual growth. And partly it was God's gift and grace."

It was just before taking final vows that he felt free and able to do whatever he wanted. Cyprian was finally at peace with himself. "But then I felt my true calling was to be a monk. So I decided to take final vows and continue in this life."

As we talk, he appears to grow more comfortable with my questions. But he does not look physically relaxed. The over-stuffed chair where he sits is inadequate to accommodate his long frame. His arms and legs hang out over the chair.

I ask if there have been other significant mileposts in his spiritual journey. "Yes!" he responds emphatically. "My ordina-tion into the priesthood, which took place a couple of years af-ter final vows."

Soon after ordination he was sent to study in Rome for two years in the early 1960s. New Melleray needed degreed teach-ers to instruct fellow monks. There Cyprian shared a large res-idence with other Trappist monks and faculty members from all over the world. "We were trying to live the Trappist tradition,

Father Cyprian

and go to the university and live a student life, as well," he says. "So it was quite stressful."

Prior to going to Rome, Cyprian had lived the traditional Trappist life: separation from the world and complete closure. In Rome, he was thrust into the academic world with other students, not all of whom were Trappists. "Many of the Trappist students weren't ready to live with one foot in the world and the other in the monastic tradition," he remembers. "As a result, one third of the students left the order, another third stayed and became leaders, and the final third became rank-and-file teachers."

By the mid-1960s, he had been sent to Assumption Abbey. Traditionally, a Trappist monk remains in the monastery where he has taken his final vows, but there are exceptions to the tradition. One exception is when a monastic community establishes a new foundation, called a "daughter house," and sends some of its members there to assist.

"In the early years of a new foundation there are always monks moving back and forth because of special needs. They may need a carpenter or teacher or some other person with a particular skill," explains Cyprian. In his case, Assumption Abbey needed a qualified priest to teach an introductory scripture class, and Cyprian was asked to do it.

Initially, the understanding was that Father Cyprian would only stay for the summer. But the summer was extended into a year, then two, then three, until he became an integral member of Assumption Abbey. "I had lived here long enough with the other men and I was happy here," he says, smiling. "They were willing to put up with me and I was willing to put up with them. So I decided to stay, and they voted me in." If he hadn't been voted into the community, Cyprian would have returned to New Melleray.

"I have been the abbot here going on five years," he says, readjusting his long frame in the chair and crossing his legs. His right leg begins to swing casually as we continue to talk.

"We have a choice now. When St. Benedict wrote *The Rule* he presumed lifetime abbots, unless there was incompetence or mismanagement. Since Vatican II, each community has the authority to decide whether or not their abbot will have an unlimited term." Assumption Abbey monks voted to select an abbot for a six-year term.

In October 1962, Pope John XXIII convened the Second Vatican Ecumenical Council in Rome. There would be four sessions before the council concluded three years later. Prior to that, the most recent Vatican Council had been held in Rome a century before. There have been only twenty-one ecumenical councils in the history of the Church. The Nicene Council of 325 was the first.

The pope's intent was to initiate ways to renew the Church in the modern world and to promote diversity throughout its hierarchy. He wanted to involve the laity to a greater extent and to seriously consider reforms advocated by ecumenical and liturgical movements in the Roman Catholic Church worldwide. John was a breath of fresh air and a potential liberating force in an otherwise stagnant Church patriarchy. His efforts at reform were often met with resistance by conservative forces within the Church hierarchy.

In her highly informative book *101 Questions and Answers on Vatican II*, author Maureen Sullivan writes that the pope's announcement of the council was unexpected, to say the least. There was "shocked silence on the part of the cardinals themselves, who had grown used to the notion that nothing needed changing. For many of them, the church was a perfect society," writes Sullivan (p. 13). This way of thinking resulted from the First Vatican Council's declaration that the pope's teaching authority was infallible.

Pope John XXIII's efforts resulted in increased attention to underdeveloped countries and cooperation with other Christian and non-Christian religious organizations. Church practices and teachings became more accessible to the lay membership, and the Mass was to be spoken in one's native language. Of course, this renewal spilled over into all of the monastic orders, including the Trappists. Unfortunately, John died before the completion of the Second Vatican Council. In the absence of a progressive pope, very conservative Church authorities quickly regained their dominant role.

Father Cyprian happens to mention his transition from community monk to abbot. "It was rather unexpected. I was a rank-and-file monk. I didn't know if it would work out or not, but I felt that I should try." He tells me that it took him a couple of years to settle into the new routine. The added responsibilities and decision making were part of the process.

"St. Benedict pretty well sketches out the role for the abbot." He adds, smiling, "Benedict's description, of course, is impossible." Cyprian says that each man in the role will have a different style. Some men will see the role as that of a shepherd who nourishes his flock through his teachings. The abbot will guide his flock and lead the way.

"Is that how you perceive your role?"

"Well, you know, that is my viewpoint as an abbot. And, each man will do that in his own way. Ten shepherds, each guy will have his own personal touch, but Christ is always the Shepherd."

Recently, I discovered that Assumption Abbey has a daughter house in the Philippines. The new monastery has an interesting story, which the abbot shares with me. "The Philippine community was not founded by our monastery but by a group of Trappist volunteers." Four of the twelve monasteries provided half a dozen men. "We only had one Philippine monk in our entire order at the time. And he kept saying that if we would make a foundation in the Philippines, we would get vocations." Cyprian's excitement about the recently established community is obvious. He sits up in his chair and leans forward as he tells me the story. His words come more easily, and he gestures spontaneously.

The six volunteers came to Missouri and moved into the old Assumption Abbey monastery now standing empty down the road. "They lived there for six months getting to know one another and functioning as a community before traveling abroad." Because they became a cohesive group here in the Ozark foot-hills, Assumption Abbey was asked to be their motherhouse.

The new daughter house in the Philippines is one of many Trappist monasteries in the developing world. "Following Vatican II, the Roman Catholic Church authority asked that all religious orders make foundations in developing countries," he explains. "We now have many foundations in Central and South America, and in Africa and Asia."

With obvious pride, he reveals that the new Abbot General (the international Trappist leader) is Argentine. "Now, that's a real departure from the past because Cistercians [Trappists] are French by origin and European for centuries and centuries." Cyprian stops for a moment, allowing time for a question if necessary. "But to go from European abbots, mostly French and a few English, to bypass all the monasteries in the developed world and choose an Argentine, well. . . ."

"So how did that happen?" I ask.

"The Holy Spirit!" he proclaims.

Having spent years of my life traveling and working in the developing world, I want to know more about the reality of a European-based monastic order moving into a developing country. Surely monastic life changes under the influence of different cultural and social norms. Cyprian acknowledges that it changes as it absorbs cultural differences, but, he emphasizes, the motherhouse and the foundation have chosen the same essential values. "You see, that's the marvelous work-ing of Providence at this stage."

Historically, the Cistercian Order was composed of inde-pendent monasteries governed by abbots who made the choice to unite under one constitution. The abbots, who became the governing board, would meet periodically. "They established their order and uniformity in observances so every Cistercian monastery did everything at the same time in the same way everywhere," explains the abbot. "The renewal in our order changed the focus. We now strive for a unity in essential val-ues with a legitimate pluralism in living out those values." Therefore, the Philippine Trappists' "lived experience and way of life is essentially like that of ours, but yet very different, quite different because of their culture."

He has visited the community on two separate occasions, which he is required to do as motherhouse abbot, just as the Iowa abbot must visit Assumption Abbey. "It's exactly the same," Cyprian says. "Your mother-in-law comes for a friendly visit to see how the family is doing."

Until the Philippine community was able to get on its feet financially, all twelve Trappist monasteries in the United States helped to support it financially. "Now they have fish ponds, coconut and mango orchards, and a jelly industry. All of that needs good management."

As our conversation winds down, I inquire about important community symbols. "If you were to portray your community through the use of a camera, what symbols of this life would you photograph?" The abbot sits back in his chair and looks out the window as though he's searching for the answers. He's quiet for some time before he turns back to me. There's been a transition. Once again his words are measured.

Abbot Cyprian mentions the chapel bell as the keeper of time and the church sanctuary where the monks meet for litur-gical services throughout the day. The sanctuary is such an integral part of the monks' lives. He also suggests a photograph of a monk on a solitary walk, and another of the monks gathered for a meal or in community dialogue during Chapter, the weekly community meeting. "We're called to a life of solitude always deepening, but also a life of relationships—fellowship and sharing with each other in Christ." He sits quietly for a moment and then adds, "So you have two poles: the solitary and the community."

Cyprian would also include a photograph of manual labor because it's an aspect of their tradition: supporting themselves by their work. "Traditionally, that would be a simple earthbound work, like Brother Boniface with his chainsaw in the woods." He adds, "But now we are moving into a world of technology." A final image that he suggests capturing is that of a monk reading scripture within the context of *lectio divina*, a Trappist meditative practice. It is a meditative reading of the scripture that is the threshold of contemplative life. "It is the traditional way of monks' praying," reveals Cyprian.

He explains that there are four stages in the practice. First the monk reads a selected scripture and listens to what it is saying to him in the moment. In Latin, this is called the *lectio*, or reading prayerfully. *Meditatio*, or meditation, is the second stage in the process. When a thought or a phrase stands out from the scripture, the monk begins to repeat it.

"Is it like repeating a mantra?" I ask.

"Exactly so," the abbot confirms.

"Then you move into the third stage, *oratio* [prayer]." The repetition of the words, like the chanting of a mantra, leads the monk into prayer. And the final stage, *contemplacio* [contemplation], is the process of quieting down and "simply being with self in the presence of God."

As with any deep spiritual meditative discipline, time and practice lead to a mastering of the technique. "It isn't something that one can manipulate or just make happen," he tells me. "But rather, it's a gift from God. It's kind of like the differ-ence between driving with your foot on the accelerator, and turning on the cruise control but still doing a little driving. But the thrust, the power, the engine has taken over. It is God who is there with you."

The monk just rests with God.

CHAPTER THREE

~

War No More

We do not see things as they are;
we see things as we are.

Talmud
6th Century, A.D.

The Psalms mirror our world but do not allow us to become voyeurs. In a nation unwilling to look at its own
violence, they force us to recognize our part in it. They
make us re-examine our values.

Kathleen Norris
The Cloister Walk

I am disoriented and sitting in the front pew just before Vigils
begins. The space is uncomfortably warm in contrast to my
room, where the window stands wide open. A few lights cast a
pale glow over the room.

As the monks drift into the sanctuary, their walking appears
slow and labored, single movements blending together for
completion. They are like "frames of motion," popularized by

the distinguished photographer Edweard Muybridge in the early twentieth century—detailed photographic studies of isolated movements in various stages of walking, running, and crawling.

Even my own movements feel broken into isolated frames of motion. I am experiencing an altered state of mind.

"O God, come to my assistance. O Lord, make haste to help me. Praise the Father, the Son, and the Holy Spirit both now and forever. The God who is, who was, and is to come at the end of the ages. Amen," repeat the monks in unison at the opening convocation.

I turn my head when I hear a fellow visitor. I watch as he walks forward from the rear of the sanctuary and sits down. He, too, is moving in a slow and labored manner. Without much thought, I stand up and walk out of the sanctuary. In the hallway I take a half dozen deep breaths, shake my arms and hands, roll my head from side to side a few times, and then quietly return to the pew. I recognize this altered state of mind. I experienced it once before, decades ago.

After a family visit in Kansas, I was driving through the mountains in Pennsylvania on my return trip to New Jersey. It had been a typical cross-country marathon, when eighteen-hour driving days were the norm, and a few hours of sleep at a rest stop were considered sufficient before launching off for the next day. The icy, narrow, and winding blacktop was treacherous. It was after midnight, and heavy fog embraced the road. I began to fall asleep at the wheel.

When I spotted flashing red neon lights ahead, spelling out "Smiley's Café and Motel," I turned off the highway and drove down a steep exit road into a muddy parking lot. A few long-haul trucks and pickups were parked in front of the run-down, two-story concrete-block building. The café and a repair garage were on the first floor, with motel rooms above.

As soon as I pushed open the frost-covered door and walked into Smiley's, I knew that I had entered a different dimension. It was a Brigadoon coffee shop, only to be experienced once in a lifetime. The cigarette smoke inside was thicker and more deadly than the fog outside. Golden oldies, blaring from the jukebox, were running at a speed slower than normal: 45s playing at 33-1/3 rpm. Lowering my head, I cut through the smoky room to the sparkling Formica counter and claimed a shiny round stool with a blue vinyl cushion.

"C-a-n I g-e-t y-o-u s-o-m-e c-o-f-f-e-e, h-o-n-e-y?" asked the friendly waitress, enunciating each letter of each word. Looking six feet tall, her face dominated by rouge and deep red lipstick, the woman strode across the red linoleum floor like a slow-moving wind-up robot.

"Y-e-s, M-a-'a -m, a b-l-a-c-k c-u-p o-f c-o-f-f-e-e w-o-u-l-d b-e m-i-g-h-t-y g-o-o-d," I replied. "A-n-d I w-o-u-l-d a-p-p-r-e-c-i-a-t-e a g-l-a-s-s o-f w-a-t-e-r." I, too, was unwillingly enunciating each letter of each word. Our conversation dragged on, its pace slowed in my perception.

"How about a nice fresh piece of cherry pie à la mode to go with that coffee?" she asked enticingly and painfully slowly.

"No thank you, ma'am, the coffee and the water will be just fine." I had been anxious when I first walked into the café. But I soon acclimated to the circumstances and enjoyed my stay. When I finally managed to extract myself from Smiley's and walk outside, the blast of cold air snapped me out of my trance. I inhaled deeply, as if I had been holding my breath through the entire experience.

This morning's episode isn't as extreme, but I feel as though I have entered another dimension. This time I have stepped into a scenario out of the Middle Ages. Predawn Liturgy of the Hours has been a mainstay of Christian monastic life since the seventh century. The monks' reading of scripture and chanting

Liturgical hour

of psalms is interspersed with quiet intervals for silent prayer. I sit and stand at appropriate intervals with the others in the sanctuary. And I watch the monks intently.

"Do monks, or contemplatives, see the same world as the rest of us do, or are theirs different eyes?" asks Walter Capps in *The Monastic Impulse*. "Do they see the world via another mode of perception, or is it another world? Can 'an eye that is single' penetrate several dimensions, and find the perceptual basis for allegorical interpretations? That is, does interior silence give formation to its own world, and then such worlds are subsequently seen?" (pp. 17–18).

Abbot Cyprian repeats the words that close every service, "Let us bless the Lord."

"Thanks be to God," all of us respond.

The monks file out, and most of the visitors follow. I remain in the pew. Although the lights are turned off, a few candles still flicker. Matthew, who has also stayed behind, slowly walks to the railing, whispers a string of words, genu-

Brother Dominic stands in the middle

flects, and leaves quietly. This alone time gives me an opportunity to digest the liturgy and absorb the events that have just unfolded.

Soon I leave the sanctuary, push open the exit door, and spill out into the star-filled darkness. The cold air wraps around me, and I breathe it in deeply. Déjà vu. I feel as though I am breaking the surface, as if I had been swimming underwater.

"I've never seen a sky so full of stars as there were last night," Matthew proclaims when I walk into the dining room hours later. He and John, Michael, and Father Richard are huddled around a table. I'm back to operating in the present dimension. Events around me are unfolding at a normal pace. I serve myself cold cereal, juice, and coffee and join the others for breakfast.

"Did you see the stars last night?" Matthew asks excitedly, looking over at me. Before I have an opportunity to confirm last night's spectacular light show, Matthew continues, "God gave that to me for a birthday present! Seventy-eight years ago I was born." His voice is strong, and his spirits are high.

"You know, most people think of a party with presents and cake for their birthday," he says, "but the stars in the heavens were enough for me." Matthew pauses, looking at each of us directly. His voice lowers, as if he is revealing a secret. "I was high last night," he says, looking around to register our reactions. "Not on drugs or anything, but high on my relationship to God." He smiles widely, and his dark eyes twinkle. I am tempted to share my own high from early this morning, but I decide to keep it to myself.

Father Richard, usually a wonderful source of monastic stories, momentarily diverts our attention from last night's light show. He begins to tell a dramatically different story about a past visitor. It feels as if there has been a disconnect in our conversation.

"At the age of twenty-three this man was in the armed forces and serving in Vietnam," Richard begins. He doesn't reveal the man's identity. The four of us lean in closer to hear the story. "Please speak up and slow down," requests Matthew. Father Richard meets the first request, but I'm not sure that it is possible for him to fulfill the second one.

"He was in military operations where a Vietnamese ally would go into a village, identify the Vietcong or sympathizers, then leave and tell the U.S. military forces what information he had gathered," Richard continues. "The U.S. forces would then go into the village at night, interrogate the identified persons, and kill them." It was understood that no prisoners were to be taken.

This story is a familiar one. I heard scores of them from the military personnel who visited the antiwar coffeehouse outside Fort Knox. Usually the Pentagon and the White House would deny that such activities ever occurred.

Father Richard goes on, "On one occasion we asked our friend to get up and speak in the sanctuary at a special gathering. He got up and told us that he had to be the one to kill the enemy because no one else would." Richard takes a deep breath and continues. "Well, a couple in the congregation got up and walked out."

"Did they come back?" asks Matthew, looking spellbound.

"Yes, they did," he answers. "They came back under their own volition. Nobody tried to force them."

All of us sit back in our chairs and remain silent for a time. Richard's motivation for sharing this story puzzles me. My mind drifts back to that dark period of American history.

During my sophomore year at university, I enrolled in ROTC the first semester. I will never forget the Pentagon propaganda films narrated by John Wayne, which all cadets had to view. Although Wayne had never served in the military, he was useful to the Pentagon and influential with cadets and potential recruits as a celluloid hero and star of numerous Westerns and war movies. Those films were a wake-up call. It was clear to me that Wayne's film-star status was being used to manipulate the viewer and romanticize the war. During my second semester, I sought out well-informed war opposition leaders, listened to their analyses, read the books they recommended, and became convinced that the United States should not be in Vietnam.

The following year, my volunteer work at the antiwar coffeehouse in Kentucky introduced me to informed speakers, documentary war films, and discussion groups with military personnel that further confirmed my opposition to the war. And I felt called to participate in local and national large-scale demonstrations as another means of countering the deceptive and lethal policies of congressional hawks, military authorities, and the White House.

I have often pondered how unfortunate it was that my mentors, with their information and insights, weren't more readily available to the men and women who joined the armed forces, at that time, in the belief that they were fighting for democracy in Southeast Asia.

A squeak from Richard's chair breaks the now-solemn mood of the gathering. He pushes away from the table and begins to clear the morning dishes. Pastor John follows him out into the kitchen. "I don't want to bore you with my personal problems or anything, but I struggle with depression," Matthew quietly admits at the table. "I have very powerful highs." He says that he blames himself for his lows.

Matthew directs his comments to Michael, as if the conversation is a private one. Father Michael is a superb listener. The Glenmary priest has already developed a trusting relationship with Matthew. He soothes the elderly man, offering verses from the scriptures. One is Psalm 121:8: "The Lord shall preserve your going out and your coming in from this time forth, and even forever more." I memorized that one in childhood Bible school. "I have a hard time remembering the numbers of my favorite psalms, or just numbers in general," Michael admits, "but the words of the verses I retain."

I get up and clear my dishes, then return to my room. Following a long shower, I pull on a few layers of clothing and venture out into the light morning fog. I feel agitated. This morning's Vigils and Richard's recent war story weigh heavy on my mind. I walk in silence for miles.

Upon returning to the monastery, I pass Father Richard in the hallway. Earlier I had asked if we could talk about the Liturgy of the Hours in more detail. He says that he has some reading material for me. "I have a few more household duties to complete, and then we can talk."

Half an hour later, he comes to my room with reading material in hand. But before we can settle into our conversation, two automobiles drive into the parking lot, which is just outside my window. Two men and a woman get out of their cars and begin to unload them. Richard excuses himself so he can greet them, make them feel at home, and take care of their immediate needs.

"In a world in which we are so easily labeled and polarized by our differences: man/woman, Protestant/Catholic, gay/straight, feminist/chauvinist, monastic hospitality is a model of the kind of openness that we need if we are going to see and hear each other at all," comments Kathleen Norris in *The Cloister Walk* (p. 162).

I begin to review the materials that Richard left. There are seven liturgical hours celebrated throughout the monastic day. In this community, five of the Hours are observed in the sanctuary. The three major choral offices, each with a Latin name, are Vigils/Watching (3:30 a.m.), Lauds/Praise (6:30 a.m.), and Vespers/Evening, which is observed just before supper. Four additional services, the "Little Hours," include Tierce/Third Hour (7:30 a.m.); Sext/Sixth Hour (11:45 a.m.), observed just prior to the noon meal; None/Ninth Hour (3 p.m.); and Compline/Complete, which is the last service of the day. This daily prayer schedule is designed to observe St. Paul's injunction, recorded in First Thessalonians 5:17, to "Pray without ceasing."

According to Church law, every Liturgical Hour must include one of each of the following: hymns, scriptural readings, prayers, and psalms. "The psalms have been a spiritual mainstay since before the time of Christ. They were and have remained an integral part of the Hebrew liturgy and Bible," writes Frank Bianco in *Voices of Silence*. "Christ and Mary frequently used the psalms to express themselves, especially on significant occasions" (p, 106).

When I read that the chant of the Church is really sung prayer, I recall the melodious sounds of the Spanish Benedictine Monks from the Monasterio de Santo Domingo de Silos. Their recording of *Chant* helped reawaken me to the meditative and prayerful power of Gregorian chant.

Looking up from my desk and out the window, I notice my furry antagonist walking over to inspect the two new cars in the parking lot. Dyers slowly circles the Chevrolet, stopping at each wheel for a sniff. He chooses the right front tire, lifts his leg, and urinates on it. Then he trots over to the Buick and repeats the ritual. This time the left rear wheel is his choice. The dog is clearly manifesting his territorial instincts.

Farley Mowat's semiautobiographical book *Never Cry Wolf* addresses this instinctual ritual with humor and insight. Mowat, a respected Canadian environmentalist and talented storyteller, writes an extraordinary account of a wildlife biologist who braves the harsh conditions of the Arctic to study the daily habits of wolves. The first significant aspect of wolf behavior that he recognizes is their use of urine as a means of declaring territorial boundaries. For his own protection, the biologist follows the animals' example and urinates a circle around his base camp. As a result, the wolves never enter his designated territory or threaten him.

Now is the time to make amends with Dyers, in the daylight. Quickly exiting out the side door, I walk to the parking lot and make my appeal: "Dyers! Come here, boy. Come on!" He responds with a hostile growl and stands his ground. I move closer and kneel down in a less threatening posture. "Take it easy, boy." A more menacing growl indicates that I'm getting nowhere. I throw up my hands in frustration and return to my room and my research.

"Leave some room for birthday cake," whispers Michael, stopping me in the hallway following midday prayer. "We're going to celebrate Matthew's birthday." (In the monastery, monks don't celebrate their birthdays. Instead, they celebrate their saint's days. That tradition creates a more intimate relationship between the monk and his designated saint.)

"Was this your idea?" I ask quietly as we serve ourselves from the buffet of baked chicken, green beans, and coleslaw.

"The idea was supported by several people in the community," Michael whispers back.

The newly arrived female visitor isn't in the dining room. But the two men, owners of the recently marked Chevrolet, introduce themselves and join us at the table. Gregarious and talkative, Larry and Scott are seniors and a longtime couple from St. Louis. Periodically they come for weekend retreats, but this visit is only for a day.

As we eat and talk, Matthew stands up and wishes us peace and joy on this glorious day. "I want to thank all my brothers here at the table for being present on the day of my birthday." We applaud as Matthew acknowledges each of us. "It's the best birthday I've ever had," he says, and returns to his seat to finish the meal.

Father Richard and John make a casual exit to the kitchen and return minutes later carrying a layer cake with white frosting. Lit candles decorate the top. We spontaneously begin to sing "Happy Birthday" to Matthew, and although he tries to contain his emotions, tears run down his cheeks.

"Blow out the candles," says someone at the table. Matthew takes a deep breath and blows them out. But a cluster of them begins to flicker again. Matthew takes another deep breath and blows out the flickering candles, but they immediately reignite.

"I'll bet Father Richard is responsible for those candles," declares Michael. It's exactly the kind of good-humored prank that Richard would pull.

"Don't blame me," Father Richard says with a grin as the still-burning candles transform into mini-sparklers. We laugh so hard that a few of us, including Matthew, have a difficult time catching our breath. Richard persistently refuses to claim credit for the "eternal flames." So Matthew declares them the work of the Lord and leaves it at that. Richard returns to the kitchen and comes back with a large pair of metal tongs. "I used to operate a crane elevator," he announces. With great precision he extracts the glowing sparklers from the cake.

"Monasteries are a great treasure in society, a very rich kind of place," comments Abbot Stephens in Frank Bianco's *Voices of Silence*. "There's a spectrum, a certain richness of personalities. There is a space for a great variety of personality and values, art and work, approaches to God" (p. 202).

As we finish our cake, Father Michael announces that he is going to say the stations of the cross and invites Matthew to join him. "Sure thing," replies the birthday celebrity. "I'll just be a minute while I get my coat."

I follow the two men outside, but as they walk toward the first station, I veer off onto the narrow trail that snakes its way down to the stream. Patches of velvety green moss and lichen cover the path and create a cushion beneath my shoes.

Off in the distance I notice Pastor John up on an embankment across the stream. Perched on a fallen tree trunk set back in the woods, he sits reading from a thick volume covered in red cloth. I respect his solitude, remain silent, and continue to hike down the winding stream deeper into the woods.

It's unseasonably warm this afternoon, and I begin to shed my clothes—first the green vest and then the blue turtleneck shirt. Without a second thought, I sit down and remove my shoes and socks and roll up my pant legs. Dead leaves crunch under my feet, and I feel the sensual softness of moss-covered rocks. Myriad plants look as if they are about ready to blossom.

Nature is playing a trick on them with this warm weather. I wallow in the unexpected lushness of my surroundings.

With clothes in hand, I continue my journey, crossing the stream time and again as it intersects the path. The water gets deeper, and the stream begins to widen. When I attempt to cross on a fallen tree truck, I lose my balance and slip into the cold, shallow water, triggering memories of Bolivia.

Years ago I joined a small group for a weeklong trek on the Bolivian Inca trail. Two of us were experienced hikers, and the others were relative newcomers to the sport. We were all participating in the Maryknoll lay volunteer training program based in Cochabamba, Bolivia. The Maryknolls, a Catholic order of priests, sisters, and lay volunteers, have been community activists throughout Latin America for decades. At the conclusion of our training, my fellow hikers would be assigned to South American projects, and I would return to Central America as a freelance volunteer.

The four of us were discouraged from making the trip due to reports of political conflicts in the mountains, but we were determined to make the journey. Although we began in the blustery cold and snowy high altitudes near La Paz, our destination would take us into the steamy Bolivian jungles where the native coca plants thrive.

On our third day, following a strenuous and demanding climb, we confronted a deep, wide mountain stream in which rushing water foamed around sharp-edged boulders. The traditional extended swinging bridge shown on our primitive map was no longer there. In its place was a very long and narrow tree trunk precariously balanced between the stream's banks.

First we tried to cross individually. But after an unsuccessful attempt, when one of us almost slipped off the moss-covered trunk into the rushing waters below, we decided upon another plan. Removing our backpacks, we formed a line of bodies and equipment and successfully reached the other side by slowly scooting across on our behinds.

This Ozark brook is but a trickle of water compared to the raging Bolivian stream. But my present circumstances frequently connect with my past experiences when I am on a retreat. I can see more clearly in this environment, more easily connect the dots in my life.

Walking back, I marvel at the long-legged insects that dance across the surface of the water, swat at the tiny black gnats that swarm around me in cloud clusters, and listen to the birds' melodious conversations in the treetops above. All of God's critters are acting as though spring has arrived.

I encounter John again. He has progressed farther down the valley and now sits closer to the stream. This time he looks up, and we exchange a silent salute as I pass by. Except at mealtimes, we try to honor the keeping of silence.

Late in the afternoon, I return to the guest library and discover a pamphlet titled "Our Lady of the Assumption Abbey," hidden behind dust-covered hardbacks. There is no recorded author or copyright date. The pages are unnumbered. Father Richard later tells me that it was written in the early 1960s, before Vatican II. I take it back to my room, sink into the overstuffed chair, and begin reading. Although outdated, it reveals a period of monastic history and offers further insight into the lives of the men at Assumption Abbey.

According to the booklet, a businessman from nearby Springfield approached the abbot of New Melleray in Iowa with the idea of establishing a Trappist monastery in the Ozark foothills. The businessman was willing to donate extensive land holdings in the area, provided that the monks would agree to never divide the rural property into parcels and sell them. An amicable agreement was reached. In September 1950, the first abbot of Assumption Abbey and his New Melleray recruits arrived here and established a new foundation. In the following weeks, months, and years, additional New Melleray monks were enlisted as reinforcements.

In their first winter, the monks had no electricity, central heating, or adequate food supply. They lived in a stately multistory home, nicknamed the "Swiss chalet," which the businessman had built but abandoned before completion. His wife had refused to live in rural isolation without all the amenities of urban life.

Within the first two years, the pioneer monks had planted vineyards and gardens and acquired cattle with the hope of surviving by agricultural means. Unfortunately, a drought had begun just when they arrived. As vineyards dried up, pasturelands lay sun-scorched, and extreme heat sapped the monks' energy, they experienced second thoughts about the location of their new abbey. Numerous grass and forest fires further tested their resolve. They seriously considered closing the community.

But exactly four years after the monks arrived in the Ozarks, the rains came. The land sprang back to life, and the men regained their confidence, energy, and hope. Two years later the monastery began to accept novices, and the community was recognized as an abbey—a financially independent entity.

Putting down the booklet, I shuffle to the dining room and make myself a cup of coffee. No one is around. I take a few graham crackers from the metal tin and return to my history lesson.

Prior to Vatican II, Cistercian (Trappist) monasteries had two categories of monks. "There does exist within the monastic family two distinct vocations: the vocation of the Choir Religious and the vocation of the Brother Religious," explains the booklet.

The Choir Religious were ordained priests or men who aspired to be priests. They were to have completed at least two years of college and preferably two years of Latin and one year of Greek. The monastery sought out men with a "sufficient ear" for the chanting of psalms, good mental health, and "average" physical abilities. These monks were primarily responsible for the business, liturgical, and organizational aspects of the community.

The Brother Religious "also applies himself to spiritual reading, mental and vocal prayer. . . . But his great prayer is manual labor," states the booklet's abbreviated description. Although brothers were expected to participate in the Liturgy of the Hours, their manual skills were necessary for the survival of the community. "In all employments, be it on the farm, in the kitchen, forests or tailor shop, the presence of the Brother Religious transforms into a song of divine praise the most lowly of human works." Any man seeking admission as a Brother Religious had to be at least eighteen years old with a high school degree and preferably two years of college. Excellent physical health was very important.

"The Second Vatican Council, in 1965, ordered an end to this class system in the monasteries," writes Trappist M. Basil Pennington in *Monastery: Prayer, Work, Community* (p. 89). All men in Trappist communities can now simply be called Brother, but many of the priests are still addressed as Father.

Assumption Abbey's original plans included accommodations for seventy-five monks and half that number of guests. Those plans were made at a time when many of the monasteries around the country were filled to capacity. Today, the monastery operates with fewer than two dozen men.

The bell begins to ring. I close the booklet and return to the sanctuary for Compline. I purposely sit in the pew directly behind the railing and close my eyes because I want to experience this brief period of time in self-imposed darkness, neither speaking nor standing during the service.

The other guests enter quietly through the double doors in the back as the monks begin to come in from their cloistered quarters. I recognize the sound of legs brushing against habits and the complementary shuffle of footsteps. The service begins.

Unexpectedly, the sound of a woman's humming joins the chanting of the monks. I want to open my eyes and turn around to look at the new guest, but I hold to my resolve. Her clear, melodious harmonizing provides a rich overlay to the men's lower tones, heightening the clarity and simplicity of the sung prayers. She provides the duality that Father Theodore recognized in his party banner a few nights ago.

Instead of lingering in the sanctuary after the service, I go directly to the refectory to meet our new guest. But she isn't there. I hope to meet her tomorrow.

Ain't Gonna Study War No More

Gonna lay down my sword and shield
Down by the riverside, down by the riverside,
Down by the riverside
Gonna lay down my sword and shield
Down by the riverside
And study war no more.

I ain't gonna study war no more. (repeated six times)

Gonna walk with the Prince of Peace
Down by the riverside, down by the riverside,
Down by the riverside
Gonna walk with the Prince of Peace
Down by the riverside
And study war no more.

I ain't gonna study war no more. (repeated six times)

Gonna shake hands around the world
Down by the riverside, down by the riverside,
Down by the riverside
Gonna shake hands around the world
Down by the riverside
And study war no more.

I ain't gonna study war no more. (repeated six times)

⌒∞⌒ **Reflection** ⌒∞⌒

For if they live by the work of their hands, then they are
true monks as were our Fathers and the apostles."

St. Benedict
The Rule

Brother Boniface

Taking a seat in the guest parlor, Brother Boniface plants his
feet flat on the floor and rests his arms on the chair. He is short
and strong and solid. His gentle gray eyes complement his subtle and oftentimes dry sense of humor. A faded blue short-
sleeved shirt, loose cotton work pants pulled tight at the waist
by an oversize leather belt, and weathered, ankle-high boots
are his daily work uniform. Boniface speaks when spoken to;
otherwise, he is comfortable sitting in silence. His feet remain
planted, his eye contact steady. He seldom gestures. When he
walks, he strides with a sense of mission.

"It was preordained, you might say, by my way of thinking,"
he responds, when I ask how he became a monk. "When I was
in second grade my teacher, an Ursuline sister, explained the
vocation of a Trappist brother." She said that a brother focused
on the labor demands of the community, while a monk priest
was responsible for ministerial duties. "Then and there I decided that it was for me—right then and there!" exclaims
Boniface. "I wasn't a bookworm. Even in second grade you
have your own bents. So I latched on to that one."

Growing up in Oak Park, Illinois, he attended Mass daily
and kept his second-grade experience in the back of his mind.
"I gave religion a preference in my ordinary life. So that helped
me out." After completing high school, he joined the army and
received an honorable discharge at age 20. For the next three
years, he worked in machine shops and helped his dad, who

was a house painter and decorator. That's when he learned his carpentry skills.

After one of his friends joined New Melleray Abbey, Boniface became more serious about making his move. He wrote his friend an inquiry letter, and his friend responded with an invitation to join the community. "I was twenty-three when I joined."

When Boniface entered New Melleray in 1950, the distinction between Brother Religious and Choir Religious was firmly in place. This distinction would not change for another decade, with the advent of Pope John XXIII's reform initiatives and Vatican II.

"We [Brother Religious] would say an abbreviated form of the [Divine] Office. It was called 'Pater Novis.' And we would attend an earlier Mass." He leans toward me as if to share a secret. "In some places it was called the 'milker's Mass.' Hear Mass and then go do the milking." He laughs and sits back in the chair. "We wouldn't attend the conventional Mass." During his few years at New Melleray, Boniface had various jobs: he worked as shoe repairman and assistant infirmarian, as well as farm laborer and community cook. Back then, there were almost a hundred men at the Iowa monastery.

"I came down to the Assumption Abbey with Father Theodore in 1954," he says. The New Melleray abbot sent scores of novices to the new Missouri foundation. Boniface was asked to come here because of his wide range of work skills, and he quickly adjusted. "The smaller community was more comfortable for me. It was less institutional."

When Brother Boniface arrived in Missouri, he was assigned to help care for the vineyards and the fruit orchards that had been planted a few years before. The monks sold their peaches and apples locally and in nearby Springfield with the help of local TV advertising. "We had two kinds of grapes, Catawba and Concord," he says. "The Concord grapes were sold to the Welch's Company and the Catawbas went to Meyers, a maker

Brother Boniface and Dyers

of champagne." For a dozen years, the fruit orchards and vine-yards provided income for the community.

"The reason we got out of the fruit business was because of the frosts." The community experienced "killer frosts" two out of every three years. Beyond commercial concerns, the monks' own food supply was affected. The frosts reduced the harvest from their community garden. For a quarter of a century, the garden produced an abundance of vegetables for the monks. But it was discontinued when the manpower demands became too great.

At the same time, the monks were also raising sheep and dairy and beef cattle on their acreage. Boniface wasn't directly involved with the animals. "We had maybe a hundred sheep. There was a lot of shearing involved, but there wasn't much profit in it," he admits. The monks raised Jersey, Guernsey, and Holstein cows for their dairy business, and Black Angus for beef. "Black Angus was the best. But there weren't really enough to pay the bills."

When the cattle and sheep and the fruit orchards didn't pay the bills, the monks decided to build a concrete-block factory. That business would be their primary source of income for al-most two decades. Since each monastery is responsible for its financial well-being, it is imperative that each community es-tablish an enterprise that fits its needs. Over the years, the abbey's businesses have developed according to the needs and abilities of the men.

During the first few years of the concrete-block factory, Boniface was practically a one-man operation in the orchards and vineyards, except during harvest time. "Later on, I was the workhorse down at the block plant." The factory work was hard and demanded a good deal of manpower from the small community of aging men. "Some of us weren't getting any older, but some of us were," he tells me.

"Obviously, you weren't getting any older?"

"No, I wasn't," he says, smiling.

"Eventually we had to sell the block factory because there was a slump in the business," he says. "We had competition from another Missouri outfit. They lowered their prices so we had to lower ours. We were losing money on the thing."

I stop the conversation and ask if he would like to have something to drink. "Nope," he responds resolutely. "I'm just fine." However, I take a break, go get two glasses of water, return, and give him one of them. He sets it on the table, and we continue.

After the factory sale, the community lived off the profits for a time and also began to sell lumber. "The tree sales were an interesting story. You want to hear it?" he asks. I nod, and he scoots up to the edge of his chair.

"A man came in and offered $20,000 for all the pine and oak on the land. Well, I was green and I thought that was pretty good. I knew that the wood wasn't that good. But I also knew that it should be sold by the load, so I said no." Boniface becomes animated as he tells the story. "Then he came back and offered us $50,000. And I still said no. Then he offered $55,000. And I said no again." He pauses. Here comes the finale. "So, I offered to sell it by the load and got $86,000."

"Now, I think the man was honest," concedes Boniface. "He was just a good businessman." It sounds to me as though Boniface was the good businessman.

Because he was directly involved in the initial timber sales, Boniface eventually became the community woodsman. Practically every afternoon he heads out to the woods with a chainsaw and Dyers, his companion. The community has three thousand acres of timberland. "I thin a little less than an acre a day. At the rate that I'm cutting, it will take twelve years to make a complete round." The remaining four hundred acres of pastureland are leased to the neighbors.

Boniface says that his first complete round of thinning the woods took longer because it hadn't been done since the Indians owned it. "People before me didn't have chainsaws," he explains. "They would go through and cut the trees but leave a lot of junk. There are a lot of good trees out there, and with proper thinning they will get stronger."

In the Ozark foothills, the dominant natural wood is walnut. Boniface says that the shortleaf pine, native to Missouri, also grows abundantly in this area. I tell him that I haven't talked this much forestry since I was a woods worker myself. Boniface smiles and says, "Hardest labor you ever did, right?"

"You're right, it was."

I explain that I was a member of a tree-planting cooperative in Oregon. "We had eight different crews that would bid planting contracts with the National Forest Service and share the profits. Each crew was unique and given a descriptive name. My crew's name was 'Red Star,' and we were very active in environmental and political issues." In the summer, our crews would bid on contracts for trail clearing, pinecone picking, and fire fighting.

Besides being the one-man forestry crew, Boniface is also the community cook. He isn't new to the job. Many years ago he became the keeper of the kitchen by default when a disgruntled novice, who had taken temporary vows, abruptly announced that he was leaving. Prior to his departure, he gave Boniface a two-week apprenticeship. Boniface took on the job for several years until another monk accepted the position. But when his replacement died, Boniface was asked to return to the kitchen.

He says that it is easy to balance working the kitchen in the morning and in the woods in the afternoon. "I think of the outside work as leisure time. But you might call it hard work." He adds that although cooking is light work "as long as you know how to use a can opener," it is not "all that congenial to my mentality." But cooking for large numbers of guests during the year doesn't worry him. "It doesn't take much more work to peel ten extra potatoes."

Boniface doesn't wait for me to end the interview. Rather, he abruptly jumps up and points to his watch. "It's almost 1:00. I've got to make sure that everything is in order for the work afternoon." We shake hands, I thank him, and he strides out the door on the way to his next mission.

CHAPTER FOUR

Silence Spoken Here

It is simply that silence is to be cherished;
it is the contemplative's fundamental raw material.

Walter Capps
The Monastic Impulse

The experiences called to mind here
were born in the desert
that we must not leave behind.

Albert Camus
The Myth of Sisyphus

"We have come here tonight to propose that the city council desig-nate a mutually agreed-upon amount of money to renovate the con-demned one-story home on University Avenue and Williams Street." I pause to look at each member of the city council and then continue. "In that building we wish to establish the first 'House of Silence' in the country." This is the council's regular Monday night meeting, which is open to the public.

Behind me sit representatives of many local religious and spiritual organizations cosponsoring the proposal.

"What exactly is a House of Silence?" asks one of the female council members.

"A House of Silence is a quiet space available to anyone who is simply seeking a place to pray, meditate, or think," I respond. "It is a sanctuary open to the general public for brief periods of personal retreat. In our noise-filled culture, there are few places of quiet where people can go and simply be with their own thoughts."

"Who will be able to make use of the facility?" asks the council chair.

The Buddhist representative, Ginny, stands to answer her. "It will be open to anyone age sixteen or older. We feel that someone that age can be mature enough to use the facility wisely and with respect."

Another council member asks if one particular church or spiritual organization will be responsible for the House of Silence. Speaking on behalf of the local mosque, a woman named Ibtisam explains that all sponsoring groups will work cooperatively to maintain the house.

A young priest from the Catholic Newman Center on the university campus adds, "You see, the responsibility for the House of Silence will rotate from week to week or month to month, depending on what we decide."

The youngest member of the council, an attorney, inquires about the interior of the building. He wants to know what religious symbols will be represented there. I motion for the Unitarian-Universalist representative to take that question.

"Mr. Councilman, there will be no religious symbols, paintings, or literature available in the House of Silence." George's answer surprises some of the audience members, and quiet chatter breaks out in the chamber. He continues, "If individuals desire religious literature and symbols they can find those things in their respective religious communities. What we are proposing is an interfaith place of quiet that is open to anyone regardless of religious affiliation."

"Do you have an interior design for the building?" asks another council member, a real estate salesman.

"Yes, we do," I reply. "The primary space, with windows on two sides, will have a simple altar in the middle of the room. Chairs or pews will form a circle around the altar." An African American man from a local Baptist Church adds to my answer, "There will be a small kitchen, a bathroom, and a room for the representative on duty. The house is small, an ideal size for our plan."

The final question comes from the oldest council member, a retired university professor. "Will you provide any additional services?"

"No, we will not," answers a woman active in the First Presbyterian Church. "We will take care of the grounds and keep the interior clean. She begins to sit down, then stands again to add, "Oh, yes, our volunteers will staff the building from 8 a.m. to 8 p.m. throughout the week."

"That's the final question this evening," announces the mayor. "I wish to thank all the representatives here tonight. We have a copy of your proposal. We will review it and report back to you one month from tonight. Thank you."

It is time for Mass as I complete my dream entry in the journal. Pastor John's recent comments about the House of Prayer were undoubtedly the seeds for the dream. The council chambers were familiar to me. I used to take notes at their meetings as a graduate journalism student. And I recognized the religious representatives and council members.

Arriving in the sanctuary as the service begins, I slide into an empty pew near one of the plain stained-glass windows. Father Theodore, one of the six priests in the community, is officiating.

This morning the "peace greeting," a daily ritual observed before celebrating the Eucharist, is particularly gratifying. I embrace and shake hands with as many guests and monks as I can. I want to convey, with eye contact and peace greeting, a gesture of brotherhood and a sign of spiritual solidarity.

Father Theodore lifts the chalice and repeats the words "Through Him, with Him, and in Him, in the unity of the Holy Spirit, all glory and honor is yours, Almighty Father, forever and ever." Guests join with monks in celebrating the Eucharist, the taking of bread and wine. According to the Roman Catholic doctrine of transubstantiation, the whole substances of the bread and of the wine are transformed into the body and blood of Christ during the ritual.

For me, Communion is an act of solidarity in a Roman Catholic or Protestant setting. It is a celebration whereby all participants reaffirm their religious and spiritual beliefs, the sacredness of community, and the relevance of Christ's teachings in their lives.

"Here lies the heart of ritual and even religion," says Peter Matthiessen in his afterword to David Cohen's *The Circle of Life: Rituals from the Human Family Album*. "For these rites momentarily lift us from the petty confusions of existence and makes us pay complete attention to the passage of our lives, complete attention to the human transformations that link and bind us to all other humans (as well as to the natural world), complete attention to the wonder of it all" (pp. 228–29).

The first time that I took Communion in the Roman Catholic Church was at Christmas midnight Mass. I was a high school student, baptized and confirmed into the First Presbyterian Church, swept up in the celebration, ritual, and religious theater of the event. According to Church authority, only confirmed Roman Catholics are permitted to take Communion. But in the moment, the rule was irrelevant, and I celebrated the Eucharist with the parishioners.

As a spiritual being I believe that such a significant community ritual must always be inclusive. If an individual wishes to share in this intimate act of solidarity, then I say invite her or him into the community with open arms. After my confirmation into the Roman Catholic Church, I became even more convinced that no one should ever be excluded from celebrating the Eucharist because of religious affiliation.

After Mass, I pass Father Richard on my way to the dining hall. "I haven't forgotten that we're going to meet today," he assures me. "We'll figure out a time, don't you worry."

"Which is better for you, morning or afternoon?" I ask, trying to pin him down.

"Well, the afternoon is usually better, but there might be time in the morning. We'll see." He smiles and walks away. Richard is not going to become bound by my scheduling process. There is an understanding here that things will happen if and when they're meant to happen. And the act of waiting is recognized as a worthy spiritual practice.

I am aware that St. Benedict has addressed the topic of "troublesome visitor" in his monastic code. "If in the [visiting] period he shall have been found troublesome or vicious, not only should he not be incorporated with the community, but he should even be told frankly to leave, lest others be corrupted by his ill doing." (p. 49). Most assuredly, I do not want to be a hindrance to the community.

At breakfast, I purposely sit near the female guest, a small woman with short styled brown hair. Her dark eyes communicate friendliness. She looks dressed for a walk in her long-sleeved blue pullover with matching pants and tennis shoes.

"Hi, my name is Elizabeth." She offers me a firm handshake. Elizabeth tells me that she has recently made a transition from working in hospital administration to becoming the director of a girl's college preparatory high school. "The mission of the hospital was to provide quality health care in an atmosphere of caring," she says. As part of the administration, her work was in "healing and hospitality." She adds with a smile, "I was part of the corporate conscience."

"That phrase 'corporate conscience' sounds like an oxymoron," I comment. Elizabeth smiles again but doesn't react. Instead, she begins to talk about her past.

After earning an undergraduate science degree and completing a master's degree in theology, Elizabeth felt called to join a Roman Catholic order of nuns. Her order, originally established in France, is now active on all of the continents.

"A sense of call in our time is profoundly counter-cultural," writes Walter Brueggeman in *Hopeful Imagination*. He comments that an "uncalled life" seems to be the widely accepted "ideology of our times" (p. 19).

While listening to Elizabeth, I eat as though I have just completed a strenuous physical workout. My appetite always increases on a retreat. I even excuse myself to go for seconds. After refilling my plate and coffee cup, I return to our conversation.

"One of the sisters in my order recommended coming," she says, when I ask what brought her here. "It's a time to just be; to not have interfacing with a large group. To have direction or not have direction as I choose." She sips her tea and continues, "The communal prayer here attracts me, and I appreciate the simplicity of the place. It's nearby, and I can afford it." She pauses and then completes her thoughts. "I think monks have a very important role in the Church, and I want to support them. I very much appreciate that they provide hospitality, a space to feel at home."

"In the past, I've conducted team retreats as a director," she sighs and briefly looks out the window. "But, for the last six years, I've looked for something much less structured. The group retreat does not appeal to me anymore. My need is to get away from groups." Elizabeth comments that she enjoys nature and camping retreats, where the group only comes together for morning and evening prayer. She excuses herself and goes to her room to read.

I walk out the door on my way to the chalet that once housed Assumption Abbey, which now stands in ruins. The deserted structure, less than a mile away, sits back from the county road in an overgrown field. It looks out of place. The original three-story building was made of local stone. But wooden and concrete-block extensions were added once the Trappists moved down to Missouri. Remains of one addition still stand, but the wooden dormitories have been torn down and recycled.

I begin to explore and walk up the precarious staircase that opens out into a wide interior room dominated by a large stone fireplace—one that might be found in a hunting lodge. The floors are buckled. Some of the rooms are adorned with long framed windows, while other smaller rooms, probably later additions, sit in the dark. It is a cold-looking building. Winters

"Swiss chalet" ruins

Assumption Abbey

must have been hard. The monks slept in dormitories, where they had very little privacy and few physical comforts.

Author Frank Bianco writes in *Voices of Silence* that when he was a seminary student, the Trappists were considered "the elite strike force in the spiritual life—penitents who never spoke, fasted and chanted liturgy in a way that evoked an angelic chorus" (p. xiv).

Near the old abbey stands a weathered barn constructed from stone and wood. It looks as though it were lifted out of an Andrew Wyeth painting. The structure is in good condition and still used for storage. The wood-beamed ceiling and roof are intact. Lumber, tools, and farm machinery sit on the first floor, where the smell of dried hay lies heavy in the air. Climbing up the narrow, creaking staircase into the loft, I discover iron crosses painted white. They wait to be planted in the monastic cemetery.

Death, funerals, and the loss of loved ones cloud my mind as I exit the barn, return to the county road, and unexpectedly confront a grotesquely large black SUV. Its oversized tires and imposing silver grill are like that on a diesel truck. All of the windows are tinted.

I encountered scores of these gas-guzzling monsters when I lived in Central America during the 1980s. The locals called them "deathmobiles." During political marches and public demonstrations, military personnel would sit behind the dark windows and photograph the demonstrators. The vehicles were often used by the military and the paramilitary death squads to kidnap victims off the streets or out of their homes at night. The names of the kidnapped would frequently end up on the lists of the disappeared.

The shiny SUV stops a few yards in front of me, and the operator's door swings open. "Good morning," says the driver, jumping down from the purring beast. Instead of a black beret and sunglasses, army fatigues, and a holstered gun, the urban cowboy sports a thick blond handlebar mustache, a straw hat, fancy leather boots, new blue jeans, and a white long-sleeved shirt. A woman with curly black hair peeks out from the passenger window, then quickly pulls her head back into the metal shell.

"Good morning," I reply as the military images quickly melt away.

"Say, would you happen to know where the Trappist monastery is?" he asks, hitching up his blue jeans.

"Sure do. Continue down the road a bit and then take the turn-off on your left." I point down the road. "You'll see the sign." Maybe they are taking a day's detour from Branson. The cordial cowboy thanks me for the information and returns to his mate in the monster. The tires are so oversized that he has to jump up on a step in order to crawl back in. He revs up the engine and leaves me behind in a cloud of dust.

Late for lunch, I arrive back at the monastery and discover four new visitors, men dressed in black suits with collars. They sit quietly in the dining room eating their lunch. I don't see the Branson couple.

"Those guys are Old Catholics," Father Richard tells me when I detour into the kitchen. He says they occasionally drop by for a meal. "They are a small sect that doesn't believe in the infallibility of the pope."

"Nobody believes that anymore, do they?"

"Yes, they do," he responds emphatically.

Back out in the dining room, I greet the visitors with a nod, serve myself macaroni and cheese and some salad, and join Elizabeth at the other end of the room. This afternoon our conversation focuses on Latin America. She mentions having friends who work in Peru.

"A number of women in my order are working in two different areas in the Peruvian highlands," Elizabeth reveals, expressing concern about their safety. She names the specific highland regions, and I understand her apprehension. I have traveled in those areas. The indigenous people in the highlands have been the victims of brutal attacks by the Shining Path, a Maoist insurgency organization, and by counterattacks from the Peruvian military, who perceive the peasants as collaborators. The Shining Path gains new recruits among the young in a country where political institutions are corrupt and the economy is bankrupt.

"The dilemma for our sisters is that they work in the field of public health," Elizabeth explains. "Their skills are certainly needed. But by being there, they are jeopardizing not only their own lives but the lives of the locals sponsoring their activities." The Shining Path is violently opposed to any outside assistance from religious organizations.

Pastor John joins us briefly and lightens the conversation. "I'd like to suggest that we all band together in the morning and go worship in the woods." He thinks it would be a good idea to pack a breakfast before we go. But Elizabeth and I convince him to eat first, then hike and worship together afterward.

"What's our destination?" I ask.

John holds up his hands as if he's under arrest. "I'm only the idea man. Others have to figure out the particulars. We'll work it out in the morning."

Socializing while on retreat is a new experience for me. My usual mode of behavior is silence and meditation interspersed with visits to the chapel, but I am enjoying my periods of silence and solitude intermixed with lively discussions and interactions at the dining table.

Prompted by Brother Dominic, Elizabeth and I push away from the table and share the cleanup chores. In the kitchen, I take the opportunity to chat with Dominic. "I understand that you came here from the California monastery. How long were you out there?"

"Thirty years I was out in California," he responds readily, but he wrinkles his forehead as if to say he'd rather talk about something else. "How's your foot?" he asks, knowing that I am healing from a stress fracture recently acquired while running. I tell him that the process is slow.

"I used to run," he tells me. "Now I ride a mountain bike and do sit-ups. I just recently constructed an elevated board." Dominic demonstrates the size of the contraption with his outstretched arms. He is proud of it. "I do seventy-five sit-ups a day. And I do push-ups, too." Dominic pauses for a minute to give his firm stomach a pat. "You know a lot of guys get hernias because they let their middles get soft and flabby." While I finish up the dishes and wipe down the kitchen counters, we commiserate about men's never-ending battle to keep our bellies from hanging over our belts.

Father Richard tracks me down in the visitors' library in the afternoon for our talk. We move out into the dining room where he has been making journal entries in a large rectangular hardbound ledger. He says that it serves as the monastery history book and scrapbook. "Right now I'm the monastery historian and responsible for recording community events," he informs me. "I'm way behind."

Before settling into our conversation we make cups of tea. It's quiet. The silence is broken only by the hum of the refrigerator in the adjacent kitchen. I initiate our talk by asking about the black aprons that Trappist monks wear over their white habits.

"It's called a scapular. It was originally used by the monks to protect their habits when they went out to work," explains Father Richard. The habit and a scapular had to have been restrictive and uncomfortable, not to mention hot, when working in the fields. Father Richard adds, "If a man is not wearing the black scapular, he is a novice."

In the early days, the color of the habit was of no significance. "They were always worn until they fell off," he says with a chuckle. However, the Benedictine monastic order always used black robes, which it continues to do, and thus its members became known as the "black monks." White became the traditional color of Cistercian monks' robes. "Because of our white habits, Cistercians [Trappists] were called the 'white monks.'" Richard adds that when a monk takes his solemn vows, his final commitment to becoming a monk, he receives the cowl, the hooded robe worn over the habit.

Although I have a good grasp of monastic history, I want to know more. I ask him to talk in detail about the founding of the Trappist Order, officially known as the Cistercians of the Strict Observance. "Well, in the 1600s there was a reform movement in European monastic life." He stops to sip his tea and adjust his chair. "Actually, the reformers were a few monks who happened to be studying at the University of Paris." At that time, reform meant a return to a more strict and conservative monastic practice. It was referred to as the reform of the "strict observance."

"Abstaining from eating meat was one of the major reforms," Richard tells me. He recites from memory St. Benedict's *The Rule*: "Let everyone, except the sick who are very weak, abstain from eating the meat of four-footed animals." Richard tells me that Trappists don't eat poultry either, though they do eat cheese. However, there is one exception to the rule. "We are allowed to eat turkey on Thanksgiving Day," he admits. "But I'm a dressing man." He leans back in his chair and holds his stomach. "Give me homemade dressing and gravy and I'm satisfied."

Father Richard explains that one of the smaller Cistercian monasteries called Abbey de La Trappe, in Normandy, France, joined the emerging reform movement. The title Trappist came from that community. In fact, it was their abbot who introduced another major reform: the daily practice of observing strict silence. "And there is still a strong emphasis on observing silence," I comment.

"Oh, yes," replies Richard. "Because of the strict silence, we once used a sign language to communicate. It was very similar to the language for the hearing impaired."

Richard tells me that years ago he saw a film based on Carson McCuller's book *The Heart Is a Lonely Hunter*. I know it well; the book is a favorite of mine. Two of McCuller's primary characters are men with hearing and speech impairments. Longtime friends and companions, the men live together and face the daily struggles of life. Richard says that when he watched the film he could understand the actors' signing. "It was similar to what we used in the old days."

"Did everyone have to learn the sign language when they entered the monastery?"

"Of course," he replies and sits quietly for a moment. "You could do some nasty things with it. You could tell a person to go to hell if you wanted to. In the 1950s there were rather a high number of nervous breakdowns in the Trappist Order. It was thought that a major cause might have been a lack of communication." That is when the order began to consider loosening the strict silence rules. "I found that there was a lot of nonverbal communication that became misunderstandings about very insignificant things. And they would grow and grow."

The loosening of the silence rules was actually more in keeping with St. Benedict's teachings. He advocated honoring silence in daily life, but he wasn't opposed to verbal communication within reason. Richard explains that when the rules became more flexible, the abbot began to invite men with communication conflicts into his office to try to straighten out misunderstandings. The abbot would have one man tell the other man how he felt, while the other man listened without responding. Then the two men would reverse roles. Richard says that most of the problems were resolved that way. "But that wasn't done back when I was a novice. We had a kind of 'blood and guts' approach. That was simply part of the rough way of monastic life. You just offered it up and handled it the best way that you could with charity in your heart."

This feels like a good time to break. Richard needs to make a phone call, and I want to get some papers from my room and refill my teacup. When Richard returns he has changed into work clothes. "I'm going to take a walk when we're done here," he says. I don't want to detain him much longer. I ask him to tell me about the history of the guest quarters.

"The monks and novices built it in the early 1960s," he says. "A monk came up from the monastery in Conyers, Georgia, to help do some of the block work, left when it was done, and then it sat empty for six years because the interior was not completed." Meanwhile, the monks were still living in the Swiss chalet. Eventually the community decided to build a new monastery onto the guest quarters and completed the project in two years.

The facility was built to accommodate two dozen men. "There are also two hermits in the community who live on the acreage and another monk who is serving as a military chaplain," says Richard. Although the chaplain is an ordained monk, Richard thinks that he will stay in the military and become a career officer. One other monk, suffering from Alzheimer's disease, is living in a nursing home. "The community was simply not able to give him the twenty-four-hour care that he required."

Elizabeth walks in briefly; she smiles and nods but doesn't say a word. She makes her cup of tea and leaves, honoring our conversation by remaining silent. Time and again I observe this level of consciousness and respect among both the guests and the monks.

I am not clear on the various stages to becoming a monk, and I want some clarification. "What's the first step in the information process?" I ask.

"If an interested man contacts us, we invite him for a three-day visit during the week, or for a long weekend." Richard explains that during the visit the abbot, the guest master, and one of the hermit monks will talk with him and ask some basic questions. What is he looking for? Who and what have been the major influences in his life? What is his religious and educational background? Richard says that oftentimes that brief visit makes it clear whether this life is an appropriate one for the man.

"If we give him the green light, we ask him to spend a month here and then return home for a month to think about it." At the end of that waiting period, the community writes him a letter with its decision. "If the man wishes to continue the process after the one month of observership, and we feel that he is a good candidate, then he begins a six-month postulancy."

Richard stops for a moment, casually removes his thick glasses, wipes them clean with the end of his shirttail, and slips them back on. "When the man completes his postulancy, he becomes a novice and receives the white habit." During this time, the man will live with the monks and participate in their daily routine. I know that the novitiate requires at least two years for completion and I ask Richard what the training entails.

"He will attend classes in scripture and prayer. And there will be classes focused on the Order's constitution and St. Benedict's *Rule*." The abbot will also teach the novice the practice of *lectio divina*, the method of meditative prayer that Abbot Cyprian discussed with me earlier. Meanwhile, the novice is responsible for daily labor assignments and ordinary chores. "There is really a lot to learn by just being in community. It takes time to adjust."

Richard returns to an earlier point to expand on it. "In the postulancy and the novitiate, the man can decide to leave at any time. There's no obligation to stay." However, after the completion of the novitiate and the candidate's profession of "temporary vows" or "temporary professed," he is committed to remaining in community for three years.

The guest master admits that at the end of that three-year period, some men just aren't ready to take the "solemn vows" and commit fully to this life. They're still in a state of indecision. The monk shares a story that demonstrates what he is talking about. "I knew one man who didn't take solemn vows for fifteen years. He had extended his temporary vows for six years, and then spent nine years discerning whether or not to take solemn vows." Richard does admit that if at some point a man discovers that he simply can't continue to live this life in community, there are ways to be released.

After taking solemn vows, if the man wants to study for the priesthood, he has that opportunity. For example, if a man at

Assumption Abbey chose that direction, he would probably take his training at St. Louis University or possibly at the Georgia monastery.

I have one final question for Richard. Recently, I was told that a group of women religious live as hermits somewhere on the 3,400 acres. I ask him if that is so.

Richard perks up at the change in topic. "Why, yes, yes there are," he replies. He explains that a small group of women religious living in eastern Oregon initially contacted a hermit monk at their South Carolina monastery. They wanted him to be their priest and say Mass for them daily. He liked the idea, presented their request to his superior, and received permission to do so. The group lived successfully for years in Oregon until there was an agreeable split in the community and the majority sought another place to live. "That's when they asked if they could build on our property. We took a vote and decided that they could."

There are now a half-dozen women and a priest coexisting as a community of hermits on the acreage. "They have eight or nine hermitages over there," reports Richard. I wonder where "over there" is but decide it's not relevant. "They always have someone coming in there; sometimes for a couple of months. Recently they brought a nun over from Ghana." He explains that there is only infrequent interaction between the monks and the sisters.

After I thank him for his time, Richard leaves for his daily walk, and I return to my room for a physical workout: sit-ups and knee push-ups with leg lifts and various body stretches. It's not strenuous, but it gets my blood flowing. The morning conversation with Brother Dominic has reminded me that I need to resume an exercise routine.

Before dinner, three of us join the monks for Vespers. I particularly appreciate this service because I am better able to settle down at this hour. For thirty minutes the lights are turned off, one candle flickers in the sanctuary, and there is time for reflection.

In *Blue Highways*, William Least Heat-Moon describes his experience of Vespers with Trappists in Conyers, Georgia. "There was nothing but song and silences. No sermon, no promise of salvation, no threat of damnation, no exhortation to better conduct. I'm not an authority, God knows, but if there is a way to talk into the Great Primal Ears—if ears there be—music and silence must be the best way" (p. 83).

It is during these quiet gatherings and in the prayerful silence of a Quaker meeting for worship that I sometimes experience subtle spiritual reawakenings. Quakers call it the "inner light," that of God in each of us. I am grateful to be experiencing that light in the moment.

By choice I sit alone at dinner. I want to sit quietly and fully appreciate the events of the day. After the meal, a long silent walk in the cold rain is a rewarding conclusion to the day. Without the moon lighting the way, my steps are slow and intentional.

"By now the monastery was making its way into my muscles, into my bones. I found myself walking slower, feeling taller, breathing deeper. I didn't skim; I read. My handwriting became legible," wrote *New York Times* reporter Sam Hooper Samuels in an article focused on a monastic retreat. Samuels's words capture precisely my state of being.

This Little Light of Mine

This little light of mine, I'm gonna let it shine.
This little light of mine, I'm gonna let it shine.
This little light of mine, I'm gonna let it shine.
Let it shine, let it shine, let it shine.

Everywhere that I may go, I'm gonna let it shine.
Everywhere that I may go, I'm gonna let it shine.
Everywhere that I may go, I'm gonna let it shine.
Let it shine, let it shine, let it shine.

Free of fear and hatred, I'm gonna let it shine.
Free of fear and hatred, I'm gonna let it shine.
Free of fear and hatred, I'm gonna let it shine.
Let it shine, let it shine, let it shine.

⟋⟍ **Reflection** ⟋⟍

A brother full of the fear of God should be assigned to the guest quarter. A sufficient number of beds should be made up there. And the house of God should be wisely managed by wise persons.

St. Benedict
The Rule

Father Richard

"I came from a very traditional Irish-German Catholic family in Chicago, with two older brothers and one younger one," says Father Richard. We are sitting in the guest dining room in the middle of the afternoon. He calls himself a cradle Catholic. "When I was in seventh or eighth grade they started pushing vocations. So we had priests that came into our schoolrooms and gave talks." He attended a Christian Brothers' high school and later seriously thought of joining that order. "But teaching never appealed to me," says Richard. "Both of my parents were teachers. My father loathed the job." (But years later, Richard did become a teacher.)

In his first year of high school, he read Thomas Merton's *Seven Storey Mountain*, and that was his introduction to Trappist life. "I only read part of the book because it was beyond me at the time," he admits. "But the more I learned about them the more impressed I became."

When Richard was a high school junior, his oldest brother joined the New Melleray Trappists. "My mother figured out that I was heading towards the Trappists, too, and she talked to me about it when I was a senior." He says that his other older brother was dead set against it. "My brother thought I ought to get at least two years of college under my belt, and I think he was right." However, the elder brother's opinion carried more weight. Richard completed the abbey's application, was accepted, and two months after graduating high school he entered New Melleray Abbey.

Richard pauses, leans back in his chair, and glances out the window for a moment. "Looking back, it probably would have been better to have had two years of college. But I was young, just seventeen, and I thought I knew what I wanted."

He had always felt an attraction to the religious life, but not necessarily to the priesthood. "I was an altar boy and I got to know the priest, who happened to have a drinking problem. But even before that I wasn't impressed with the priests I had met." Nevertheless, Richard eventually became a priest. "I did a year of Latin and philosophy at the New Melleray Abbey. The rest of my theology and philosophy were done at the old monastery down the road."

His life was difficult in those first few years. Once the novelty wore off, Trappist life was quite different from what he had expected. "It was tough because I was still in the throes of adolescence. But I stuck it out." Back then the postulancy lasted only one month. Today it lasts one year.

In 1953 he was asked if he would be willing to move to Assumption Abbey, and he gladly said yes. That same year, Theodore, Boniface, and one other brother volunteered to come to Missouri.

Richard was soon given responsibility for tasks that he found particularly difficult. (He doesn't say what they were.) "So if I am ever asked if vows of celibacy or charity were the most difficult, they weren't," he says. "For me, the most difficult was obedience." For five years Richard worked at a job that he didn't think he could handle. Finally, he confronted the abbot with his unsatisfactory situation. "It was amazing. The superior just pulled back completely," reports Richard, his surprise still evident in his tone and expression. "His way of dealing with me changed radically, and he admitted publicly that he had made a mistake. Anyway, I persevered."

Father Richard

He sits quietly for a moment and then he takes up a new topic. Once Assumption Abbey became an independent monastery, he could have returned to New Melleray. "I was strongly tempted to do that. But I decided not to. I took a chance." The monk smiles with resignation. "In some ways I think I made the right choice. And in other ways maybe I didn't."

His oldest brother is no longer at New Melleray. After a dozen years there, he transferred his vows to a Canadian monastery. "Up there he met a priest from the United States in an active order: teachers, social workers, and worldwide missions. He was very impressed." The brother left the Trappists and joined the other order. But he and Richard still remain in contact.

"I left the monastery in the mid-1960s myself," he reveals, saying that he felt indications that he didn't belong here. "I went to school in St. Paul, Minnesota, and then got a master's degree at Notre Dame University. Although it is fairly common for monks to take time for advanced studies, it is more common to do so in Rome. I didn't try to live as a monk on the outside of the monastery." Once he had his degrees (both of which were in psychology), he taught at a junior college run by the Holy Cross Brothers.

I express surprise that he was able to leave Assumption Abbey for such a long period of time. He says that he desperately wanted to go to school and received permission to do so from the superior. "When I finished up my studies and began teaching, I got permission to live outside of the community." He lived on the outside for nine years. "Eventually it became evident that I should come back here."

"How was it for you coming back into community?"

"It wasn't all that difficult."

Since he seems to have little else to say on that topic, I suggest that we break for a minute. He can check for messages, and I can refill my teacup and grab a few cookies from the tin that is usually kept filled for guests.

I recall an article about Richard that appeared in the *Rural Missourian*, a local monthly newspaper. It reminded me of the lighter side of him—the man who always has a joke to share. "For Father Richard Fox the attitude and life of a monk is something that shouldn't be taken too seriously all the time," the article begins. "A monastery is, after all, just made up of people—even if those people do wear uniforms and crawl out of bed at 3:15 in the morning to say prayers. He [Father Richard] has just returned from his two mile run. Monastic life hasn't squelched his love for staying fit" (pp. 4–5).

In a moment, Richard rejoins me at the table, and we continue our conversation. "A monk doesn't live this life just for the sake of being a monk," he begins. "Contemplative life is a life of prayer. You have your own type of prayer that you have to develop by yourself." He says that if a man comes into the monastery solely for community, he will quickly realize that it is flawed like any other community. "But if you have come to develop a life of prayer and an intimacy with God, chances are you will be successful."

Richard informs me that he is not only the guest master, but also the novice master. "What I tell the younger men coming in here is that we can offer them a real challenge." Because of his own trials and tribulations as a novice, he shields the new men from certain jobs. "I tell the novices that if there is anything they have been assigned that is too difficult, they need to make it known." That is what Richard failed to do for five years out of a perceived sense of obedience and obligation. "If you don't say anything about it, no one else is going to speak up," he adds.

I tell Father Richard that last night I found a copy of M. Basil Pennington's book *Monastery* and skimmed through it. In one section of the book the author compares large and small monastic communities, examining the drawbacks and benefits of both. It reminded me that many jobs must be divided among few men here at Assumption Abbey. I ask him to comment on the demands of a small community.

"Oh, I will take a small community over a large community any day," he responds without hesitation. "You tend to become quite a homogenous little group like we have here. I feel that we have really come together." Richard says that the closeness is desirable, though it can create problems for a younger man coming into such a tight-knit group. "In a big community you really don't get to know many other people. In the old days when I was at New Melleray and silence was observed throughout the day and night, there were people in the monastery that I never knew, the entire three years that I was there."

His last comment easily leads into my final question. I ask Father Richard what recommendations were given to the abbey by the Iowa Trappist abbot and Trappistine abbess during their recent visit.

He takes a moment to collect his thoughts. "It was suggested that we begin to incorporate an ongoing process of dialoguing in order to deal with some of our communication problems. And that we continue the process until it is no longer needed." As there is the power of silence, so is there the gift of the spoken word.

CHAPTER FIVE

~

Lay Down My Burden

God is then the Seer
and the Seeing and the Seen.

> Thomas Merton
> "On the Monastic Life"
> (Pennington, 1990)

Life must be lived forward,
but understood backwards.

> Søren Kierkegaard
> *Journals and Papers*

A new guest sits at the breakfast table participating in an animated conversation with John, Elizabeth, and Michael. The man has a Canadian accent—British Columbian, I'd say. On two occasions I have hitchhiked across Canada, and I have come to appreciate the range of accents found in its expansive provinces.

"I came through Kansas City and was on Prospect Avenue—tough neighborhood, heh," says the newcomer, looking around to the others for confirmation. I pull up a chair and join them.

"Anyway, I stopped for gas, and some folks pulled up beside me and said I better watch my step in that area. They had noticed my Canadian license plate." He interrupts his story, turns to me, and extends his big hand across the table, "Hi, my name is Frank. I'm from British Columbia."

"Glad to meet you," I reply. "My name is Bill, and I'm from Missouri."

Frank appears to feel right at home. He sits with his legs casually stretched out and crossed under the table. His strong angular features and brown eyes, thick dark hair, and dark skin make him stand out from the rest of us. I sense an underlying intensity in Frank, bringing to mind a city beat cop. His eyes remind me of those in news photographs of Frank Serpico, the New York City police officer famous for fighting corruption in the NYPD.

"There are a lot of drugs in that area," Elizabeth says knowingly. She has recently moved to the city.

"I guess so, heh," Frank responds, looking back at her. "When I drove up to the station there was a guy next door— looked like he was selling on the street. When he saw me, he ran away."

Frank tells us that he has a business back in British Columbia called Salty Dog Carpentry, but he is considering joining the monastery. He sent an inquiry letter to the Assumption Abbey monks, and they invited him to visit for a week. As a potential novice, Frank will spend time talking with the monks and learning more about their way of life.

St. Benedict addresses visits of potential brothers in *The Rule*. His recommendations differ considerably from contemporary practices. "Do not grant newcomers to the monastic life an easy entry, but, as the Apostle says, test the spirits to see if they are from God (1 John 4:1)." Benedict continues, "Therefore, if someone comes and keeps knocking at the door, and if at the end of four or five days he has shown himself patient in bearing his harsh treatment and difficulty of entry, and has persisted in his request, then he should be allowed to enter and stay in the guest quarters for a few days" (p. 46).

Frank reveals that his interest in monastic life began in high school. "When I was seventeen, I went to the Trappist Genesee Abbey in upstate New York and stayed for a few days. And I worked in their bakery," he tells us. "After the retreat, I wanted to stay longer, but the monks shook my hand and pushed me onto the bus heading back home. I was still in high school and living with my parents." Within the last two years, he says, he has had a "spiritual reawakening." He believes that God is calling him to the monk's life.

Pastor John joins in the conversation and inquires about Catholic vocations by asking Michael if Glenmary priests, like monks, take a vow of poverty. They don't, Michael says. "If we inherit money from the family, we can keep it." He pulls on his beard for a moment, chuckles, and then continues. "However, we can't spend more than $9,000 on a car. That's the reason that I have that big old station wagon out there in the parking lot." It also serves a second role as a bus for the kids in his parish.

Elizabeth enters the conversation and mentions a significant change in her order since she joined. The sisters no longer have to live in a traditional convent or a large household. "Once I make a permanent move to Kansas City, I will be living with my mother, who is eighty-six years old," she tells us. "Mother is also a member of my order."

Elizabeth's mother must have taken the vows of an oblate—a member of a church-sanctioned association of lay people affiliated with Catholic orders of monks and sisters. An oblate participates in a period of study and preparation required by her respective order. The preparation culminates in an act of oblation—a rite whereby the individual commits herself to applying the order's principles to her own life. I think of oblates as a monastery's extended family. Writer Kathleen Norris, active in her hometown Presbyterian church, is an oblate of a Benedictine monastery in North Dakota.

Pastor John asks Elizabeth if she plans to retire at her order's facilities. She shakes her head vigorously. "I can't think of anything worse than living in that kind of environment." Elizabeth says that she loves her order but that she simply couldn't live within the confines and restrictions of such a community.

When John, Elizabeth, and Michael begin to share stories of Catholic and Protestant missionary efforts, I turn to gaze out the windows. My imagination conjures up missionary stereotypes. Elmer Gantry, the larger-than-life character in Sinclair Lewis's book by the same name, is the first to come to mind. Gantry, a philandering, greedy, and manipulative small-town minister, becomes a spiritual con man and later an evangelist and tent revivalist. In today's media-saturated world, he would be a successful television evangelist.

Gantry fades out, replaced by the image of Nathan Price, the fundamentalist Christian missionary in Barbara Kingsolver's *The Poisonwood Bible*. Mr. Price takes his reluctant wife and four daughters to the Belgian Congo, intending to convert the indigenous people to Christianity. Instead, because of his blind self-righteous behavior and total ignorance of and lack of respect for the native culture, Price becomes responsible for the disintegration of his family and the alienation of the villagers.

I have witnessed scores of Christian zealots and their organizations in many cultures and countries. Their modus operandi assumes that all other religions are either preliminary or preparatory to Christianity. A friend of mine, who is employed by an international aid organization, refers to them as religious imperialists.

I have also had the privilege of working with representatives of faith-based aid organizations that honor and respect the people with whom they work. Their intention is not to convert but rather to offer an example of Christ's teachings through their aid and assistance. They model the passage in Matthew 22:35–40: "'Master, which commandment is greatest?' Jesus said to him, 'Thou shalt love the Lord, thy God, with thy whole heart and thy whole soul and thy whole mind. This is the greatest of the commandments and the first. And the second, its like, is this, Thou shalt love thy neighbor as thyself.'"

Monastic life rejects the "conquer and convert" interpretation of the Spirit. I believe that monks make witness through their lives, as well as their words. Men and women frequently feel called to this life of silence, prayer, and work. Their spiritual journey is usually a personal decision guided by faith, not one imposed by an outside force. For me, Christian monks can be spiritual guides, as can Buddhist masters and Sufi teachers, Hindu holy men and women, weighty Quakers, and insightful rabbis.

The monks represent a spiritual and religious model under the umbrella of the organized church, but their beliefs are not imposed on the visitor. Trappist hospitality extends to people of all faiths, Christian and non-Christian, and to people of no declared faith. "It's an environment that is impossible to manipulate," said my friend Rocket, the hard-living musician and born-again Christian. "They allow you to hang or toe the line. I've gone there to participate in the services and do manual labor with the monks."

In the silence of a Quaker meeting, I find a spiritual environment like that of the monastery. I can join with others to explore my relationship with self, with community, and with the creative Spirit. "Be still and know that I am God" (Psalm 46:10). Quakers, like monks, do not proselytize. Their lives are examples of their religious values. And Quakers, like monks, believe that they have been called to their spiritual way of life.

"For Quakers, wisdom begins in silence," says Robert Lawrence Smith in *A Quaker Book of Wisdom: Life Lessons in Simplicity, Service, and Common Sense*. "Quakers believe that only when we have silenced our voices and our souls can we hear the 'still small voice' that dwells within each of us—the voice of God that speaks to us and that we express to others through our deeds" (p. 3).

Because of last night's rain, nobody at the dining table is interested in the hike or the group worship proposed by Pastor John yesterday. Elizabeth appears pleased with the trip's cancellation. I'm not surprised, given her earlier comment: "My need is to get away from groups on retreat." But despite the fine, cold drizzle, I'm determined to take a hike.

Just as soon as I exit the guest door, Dyers walks up behind me. The long, matted black-and-white fur hangs from his bony frame, water dripping from it. The dog's wagging tail raises my hopes for a relationship breakthrough. I squat down, clap my hands, and make an appeal. "Dyers! Come here, boy! Come on, Dyers!" He doesn't move. I stand, and his tail snaps down between his legs.

"All right, don't be friendly," I tell him, and I walk away. The dog's rejection bothers me. I usually have great rapport with animals. I turn back, but he's gone.

As I splash down the county road, water drips from the end of my nose, unprotected by the poncho. Each day nature's colors change in the woods. Today it is even more dramatic because of the heavy moisture and the diffuse light. Greens are brilliant; the evergreens vibrate. And shades of browns are warm and rich. The air's scent is confusing: it recalls winter and promises spring.

"Needs, not wants, become primary, and primary needs become perceptible. Thoughts become transparent," writes Walter Capps in *Monastic Impulse*, describing a retreat transformation. "Urges and wishes are vivid. The eye desires to become single again. One is able to listen for the bird song. And notice the detail of a flower. One finds oneself making resolves to live quietly and simply, not ostentatiously" (p. 9).

Breaking into song, I entertain the giant, overhanging trees and the unseen wildlife with a rendition of Susan Osborn's "Oh, Lay Down Your Burden." It's a bluesy, spiritual number, like gospel. Her lyrics invite me to lay down my burden, pick up my light, and place it before me, then walk through the door and face my fears. The singer's influential words encourage me to sing and dance to my own music and reclaim my spiritual self.

Osborn sang this song in the first Winter Solstice Concert held at New York City's Cathedral Church of St. John the Divine, which will be the largest Gothic cathedral in the world when finally completed. She was a member of the Paul Winter Consort, the artists in residence. On that icy, snowy night, the medieval-looking cathedral overflowed with humanity. An eager audience crowded into the pews, spilled over onto the floor, and squeezed into the intricately carved wooden choir stalls near the altar.

That year had been a difficult one for the collective New York City psyche. There had been several high-profile murders, a debilitating summer "brownout" with riots, transportation and garbage strikes, and violent racial conflicts in the boroughs. I, along with thousands of others, was seeking spiritual relief. We wanted the musicians to feed our spirits, and lift us up and out of our malaise. We were not disappointed.

Osborn began the concert, sweeping down the center aisle wailing the words from "Oh, Lay Down Your Burden." Her commanding presence, full-bodied voice, and emotional lyrics raised our spirits up into the vaulting, through the slate roof of St. John's, and into the heavens. We cried and laughed and stood in awe as the music filled the cathedral with joy. The event was cathartic and spiritually stunning.

Finished singing, I am aware of how wet and cold I feel. I decide to return to the monastery. But instead of walking forward, I walk backward.

"What are you doing?" The voice belongs to Matthew. He has spotted me. I haven't seen him for more than a day.

"Walking backward," I reply.

"Why are you walking backward?" he asks.

"Well, I want to see if I observe things differently," I tell him.

"I understand," says Matthew. "I tie my shoes starting with the left foot sometimes just to observe how I approach it."

There isn't any talk about our resumes or political philosophies; we simply talk about looking at things differently. He is leaving for home after lunch. "I need to get back to my wife. She's not in very good health."

"Do you think you will make another retreat in the future?" I ask out of curiosity.

"I don't rightly know," Matthew replies. "But this retreat sure has helped me out in a lot of ways."

We say our good-byes and shake hands, and I head back to the abbey, still walking backward.

"You know what I appreciated the most?" Matthew yells and waves from a distance. "Everyone treated me like a brother."

In my mind, I carry Osborn's song into midday prayer. I slide into a front pew. The sanctuary feels inviting. Even the drone of the ceiling fans provides comfort. I watch Brother Dominic casually shuffle into the sanctuary. But before he sits down, he spots a dead insect on the sanctuary floor, walks over to it, and gives it a good swift kick, and it disappears from sight. Then he slowly makes his way to the chair, sits down, and looks straight ahead.

Midday prayer

"I looked at the faces. Quietude. What burned in those men that didn't burn in me? A difference of focus or something outside me? A lack or too much of something?" asks William Least Heat-Moon in his recollection of a monastic retreat recorded in *Blue Highways*. "To my right sat a monk transfixed, eyes unblinking and his lips, the tiniest I'd ever seen on a man, never moved. I thought if I could know where he was, then I would know this place" (p. 83).

James and Hans, two new guests who plan to spend a few days, join us for lunch. Both men have gray hair and are probably in their late fifties. They look like businessmen, casually dressed in slacks with sports shirts, comfortable dress shoes, and loose-fitting jackets. Hans, who is from Arkansas, sports a neatly trimmed moustache. Clean-shaven James lives in northwestern Missouri. They tell us that they have been close friends for years.

As we eat, they pelt us with questions, fast and furious, without taking time to digest the answers.

"How long do you plan to stay?"

"Are you enjoying it?"

"Are the monks approachable?"

"Did you come alone?"

"Have you been here before?"

"Do you have to follow their schedule?"

They don't seem to understand that the rest of us have had a few days to slow down. We're operating at a slower speed than they are. Or maybe their questions are simply a release of nervous energy. Perhaps it is a businessman's way of breaking the ice.

After the meal, Father Richard brings out an aerial map of the monastic property, at the new visitors' request, and unrolls it on the cleared table. "This is the rock quarry, you see?" says Richard, pointing to a circled area. "And if you follow this path it will take you near Father Robert's hermitage." I follow his finger as it moves across a previously marked blue line. I plan to walk to the hermitage in the next day or so. "See this meadow?" he looks up at us. "You can get there by following this path off of the main road. It's a nice spot." The property is a hiker's paradise.

Although it is getting colder outside, the rain has stopped, and I leave the building to wander toward the river in search of the hermitage trailhead. On the leisurely walk, I hear a bicycle fast approaching from behind. "Wheeeeeeeee!" yells Brother Dominic as he whizzes by on his mountain bike, decked out in a white helmet and work clothes with a windbreaker and a small backpack. He soon disappears around a corner.

Near the river I discover the trailhead and consider following it despite the mud and the long string of puddles. Instead, I begin the hike back, thinking I will return tomorrow with a pair of galoshes. On my ascent of the hill, I am revisited by Brother Dominic. "Hello, Bill!" he shouts as he grunts and strains to pedal the bicycle to the top. "Hi, Dominic," I shout back. "Godspeed!" He makes it to the top without getting off the bike, something most men or women half his age couldn't accomplish.

"When Beethoven had played a new sonata for a friend, the friend asked him after the last note. 'What does it mean?' Beethoven returned to the piano, played the whole sonata again and said, 'That's what it means,'" writes Henri Nouwen in *The Genesee Diary: Report from a Trappist Monastery*. "This type of response seems the only possible response to the question, 'What does the contemplative life mean?'" (p. 21).

Near the monastery, I move off the main road into the mud and brush in search of a magnificent, brown-spotted owl that has just soared over my head. Her wingspan must be five feet. I spot the bird perched atop a broken but erect tree trunk and approach slowly, maneuvering around the underbrush. The owl's majestic-looking brown-and-white-feathered body faces east, but her head faces west, and her dark eyes track my every move. I reach the base of the tree trunk and stare back, but she ignores me. The owl is a reminder that the monks are good stewards of the earth. They are conscientious keepers of these undisturbed woodlands as a wildlife habitat.

"If the goods of the earth belong to God, then we are stewards rather than owners, called to see that they are used equally by and for all," comments W. Paul Jones in *Teaching the Dead Bird to Sing.* (p. 48)

James and I talk in the supper line as we help ourselves to the vegetable soup, bread and cheese, and cherry Jell-O. He says that he used to be a CPA and a financial consultant, as well as a computer salesman. "I was quite successful," he boasts. Hans used him as a financial consultant for years. When we sit down at the table, James informs all of us that he and his wife have recently embarked on second careers. They are studying at a Methodist seminary, working toward their divinity degrees.

"From a raging capitalist to a man of the cloth," someone comments. James smiles and nods in agreement.

"I now seek him out for spiritual guidance," Hans remarks. "He is as competent with the spirit as he was with money." Soon the conversation drops off, and we finish the meal in comfortable silence.

Late in the evening, I am reading from my poetry collection and hear a late arrival move into the adjacent room. A few minutes later, there is a knock on my door. A young man with a mop of shoulder-length brown hair, an untrimmed moustache, and bare feet greets me when I open the door.

"Hi, I'm Steve," he whispers. "Do you happen to have an extra schedule? I don't see one in my room."

"Sure, come on in," I whisper back. I retrieve an extra schedule from the desk drawer and hand it to him. "Would you care to sit down for a few minutes and talk?" He welcomes the offer and takes a seat in the easy chair.

Steve says this is his first retreat in a Catholic monastery. "Two summers ago I arranged a stay at a Buddhist center in Eureka Springs, Arkansas," he tells me. "I appreciated the retreat because nobody was shoving anything down my throat." In his early twenties, Steve works in a bookstore in a nearby city.

Steve says that he was raised in the Catholic Church but does not attend Mass anymore. He calls himself a "recovering Catholic." I ask what he means. "Catholicism hasn't even come into the late twentieth century yet," he says. "I can't relate to a church where an extremely conservative male hierarchy pulls the strings, where women are second-class citizens and the priesthood remains celibate, just to mention a few things."

Over the years I have met dozens of people who call themselves "recovering Catholics." Their stories range from abusive behavior in the classroom, the church, or the rectory to discrimination due to their gender or sexual orientation. How difficult it must be for these men and women to regard their religious upbringing as a sickness from which they have to recover. I was once in a long-term relationship with a woman who described herself as a recovering Catholic. She could not enter a church without experiencing serious stomach pains and debilitating nausea. She never told me what personal experiences caused her such serious physical reactions.

My experience has been different. But then, I didn't grow up in the Catholic Church. I was in my mid-thirties before I joined an inner-city parish in Portland, Oregon. It was a progressive, dynamic, multicultural community and an advocate of "liberation theology." In fact, the parish agreed to become a "sanctuary"—a safe house in an underground railroad—for Central American political refugees fleeing their countries' civil wars but forbidden to enter our country legally. The founders of the local Catholic Worker House, who led assistance efforts for the homeless, were active in the parish. It was there that I first experienced liturgical dance as a form of worship and realized the power of movement as prayer. The priest, the sisters, and the laity respected one another and worked together as partners in community. They struggled to make compassionate scriptural teachings come to life in contemporary America. The parish was unique, a bright light in the darkness.

"Why did you decide to come here, given your experience in the church?" I ask Steve.

"I came to experience the life," he answers. Steve sees the Trappist monastery as different from the organized church. He says that his religious and spiritual identification is still in the formative stages. "In my opinion, all religions take you to the same place," he tells me. "Christ and Buddha taught the same universal laws. Those laws are what all major religions have in common."

During his stay, the young man plans to read, hike, and maybe attend Mass. Steve compares making this retreat to taking a camping trip in the wilderness. "It's an opportunity to step back and look at my life—a chance to communicate with God."

Come By Here (Kum ba yah)

Come by here, my Lord. Come by here.
Come by here, my Lord. Come by here.
Come by here, my Lord. Come by here.
Oh, Lord, come by here.

Someone's singing, Lord, come by here.
Someone's singing, Lord, come by here.
Someone's singing, Lord, come by here.
Oh, Lord, come by here.

Someone's praying, Lord, come by here.
Someone's praying, Lord, come by here.
Someone's praying, Lord, come by here.
Oh, Lord, come by here.

❦ Reflection ❦

[T]here are anchorites or hermits, who have come through the test of living in a monastery for a long time and have passed beyond the first fervor of monastic life. . . . They have built up their strength and go from the battle line in the ranks of their brothers to the single combat of the desert."

St. Benedict
The Rule

Father Robert

"I call it a tar-paper shack," says Father Robert with a smile, as he describes his 12' × 14' wood-frame home in the woods a few miles from the monastery. He is sitting with me in the guest parlor talking about his life as a Trappist hermit. "I was given five hundred dollars to keep the place up, and I bought roofing paper and wrapped it all around." He was trying to stop the rain from leaking in. "It's done the trick," he reports. Despite the occasional leak, the inside walls and the ceiling are sufficiently insulated. "It is well constructed, but you don't want to put a square to it."

Back in the late 1960s, Father Robert and Brother Boniface built the hermitage. "He [Boniface] was doing most of the building, and I was working at the block plant," Robert says. "I would come and help him in the afternoon."

The nearly square hut has a tin roof and is partitioned into two small rooms. Inside are a large wooden desk with a battery-powered light and a wood stove that "gives good heat," a dish cabinet and a two-burner propane cook stove, a footstool, his tabernacle, and a bed. Above the bed is the blessed sacrament. The Aladdin lamp on the desk "gives about 100-watt light," says Robert. "It's a strong light." Next to the bed sits a comfortable lawn chair, a gift from a friend. "St. Teresa of Avila said that you have to be comfortable when you pray, so that's why he gave it to me." There is no electricity or running water in the hermitage. "I pick up drinking water at the monastery and use run-off rainwater to wash with."

Robert says that he comes down to the monastery every other day. He has a meal on each visit and takes the leftovers back to his hermitage for the next day. "It works out pretty good." Sometimes the hermit supplements his supplies with cans of food from the monastery pantry. His thin, ascetic-looking body confirms that his eating habits are simple and spare.

The hermit gets up at 1:30 a.m., a time when many folks in the outside world are just getting ready to go to bed. "I like to get up and have a couple of hours of quiet prayer." Robert prays on a mat in front of his homemade tabernacle. "I read the Bible mostly in the morning," he says. "Then in the afternoon I will vary my reading. Oftentimes I will read the church fathers." Presently, he is enjoying a book about church history. "It doesn't pull any punches. [The author] tells it like it is," he says, chuckling. "It almost makes you lose your faith sometimes."

When I ask, Robert describes his visits to the monastery in more detail. "I come down Sunday morning, shower and pick up supplies, and then drive back in the truck in the afternoon." He returns on Monday to help with the community laundry and on Wednesday and Friday afternoons to do book work for the community. "I balance the books. I was guided to it when I was the abbot." He just picked it up along the way. "It's really the best situation as far as I am concerned," comments Robert about his weekly schedule. "And I really appreciate that the community allows me to be in the hermitage."

"Do you find that coming into the community a few days a week provides some sort of balance?"

Robert sits up in the chair and strokes his long white beard before he answers. "Well, I find it hard to settle down when I go back to the hermitage." He looks down at the floor as if he is trying to find the right words. "I would prefer not to come into the community. But I should be making my living, too." He says that there is less distraction living here than if he tried to live the hermit's life in the outside world.

"You can't get away from it," he says. "There is just something about being in the silence." Robert has an undeniable relationship with the hermitage and the space that surrounds it, as though it is his true home. "It is rustic and rugged. I just like it."

The rustic and rugged life is not unfamiliar to Robert. He was born in northern Minnesota very near an Indian reservation. "It was rough living—nothing subtle," he reports. "And we were the only Catholic family in the area." Although his family moved into town when he was five years old, life remained simple and rustic.

Twenty years later, in 1949, Robert joined New Melleray Abbey. Two decades later his spiritual journey brought him to Missouri. "I came down for one year, as temporary help," he explains. "But that's not unusual. A temporary stay can continue until you are carried out to the grave." Officially, he is still a member of the New Melleray Abbey and could return there. "I didn't change my stability."

Robert tells me that in 1969, the year he began to live as a hermit, there was a movement of monks from the Missouri abbey back to the Iowa monastery. Because he wasn't asked to return, he decided to stay in the Ozark foothills. "I always felt that I wanted more silence and solitude. And this was a good place for it."

He explains that there was a long period of time when Trappists were not permitted to live as hermits. "Actually, 1965 was about the year that permission was given for Trappists to request life as a hermit." According to Robert, Thomas Merton was a major force in bringing about the change.

When Robert was living at New Melleray, he was always seeking more solitude. "But at that time the Carthusians and

Father Robert

the Camoldalies, more solitary monastic orders, had not been established in the United States." The Trappists were the only cloistered monastic order in the country. "I just figured that if ever the time would come, the Lord would provide. And 1969 was the time, and the Lord did provide." Robert made his request to the Assumption Abbey superior. The request was then taken to the community members for discussion, and they agreed to let him live as a hermit. Contrary to what I might have imagined, Robert says that there wasn't really much of a transition. He just felt like he had come home. "I just settled in. I realized that it was what I wanted."

A few years later, he was asked to return to the monastery to serve as the temporary abbot. Again, I comment that the transition must have been difficult. Robert tells me otherwise. "I just thought of it as God's will and just got into it," he says. "I am pretty adjustable." One year later he was elected abbot and served in that capacity for more than a dozen years. "Finally, I said, *this is it*. I didn't want to be re-elected." At that point, he says that it was very easy to return to the hermit's life. "It was like a homecoming. I could feel a sense of deep peace and quiet settle over me."

Father Robert repeats for me something he read recently that speaks to his choice of a hermit's life: "You will die stifled by comfortability and normality, choked by small joys and small sorrows." He sits up straight in the chair and begins to shake his head. "That 'stifled by comfortability'. . ." Robert breaks off for a few seconds and then returns to what he was saying. "There *is* something about comfortability and normality that stifles the spirit. There is just something about it that kills your spirit." He pauses again, gazes up at the ceiling, then looks back at me: "I just feel that there is something wrong with our culture. We are being stifled and killed by our comfortability and normality. We are just mediocre!" Then, with a big smile, he adds that normality can be useful. "It can drive you to God!"

I ask Father Robert if he ever schedules a time to meet and talk with the other hermit monk in the community, the man who serves as the priest for the women hermits. "We just meet in the monastery once in a while. I see him about once every few months and we have a little talk, not programmed or anything." He pauses and smiles again. "Nope, no planned dialogues between the hermits."

"The other day, I noticed you walking and talking with a retreat guest," I tell the hermit. "Do people often come to you for spiritual guidance?"

"Actually, that situation was God's will," he says. "It was strange how that happened." Robert explains that normally he does not give spiritual guidance. "But sometimes if I am free, I will be asked to see people." So, he met with this man every day for a week. He says that arrangement was the exception. "If people come to me, or the abbot asks me to see someone, then I will." Robert says that people who come to the monastery will want to talk about God and their prayer life. "I am only down here a few times a week, so I will see people when needed."

When I ask him to describe his life as a hermit, he answers promptly, "The thing is, to me, it is just living a life. It is a life that I have wanted, and I don't see anything unusual about it." He stands up to stretch, walks a few steps, comes back and sits down. "To me, my life is just so natural. Any other life would be unnatural."

He adds that it is the same with prayer. People want to know how to pray. "You don't teach a child to love its mother. She just does it." He shrugs his shoulders and raises his bushy eyebrows. "You just have to be present to Jesus and realize God's love for all of us. You are just talking to someone you know, and you want to love that person."

"But it is a discipline, isn't it? I mean, it's not simply a matter of sitting down and doing it."

"It is a certain discipline," Robert admits. "You have to know God." It is important to sit down, read about God, and then reflect on what you have read, he tells me. I suspect he is talking about the Trappist practice of *lectio divina*. "It is hard for a person to just come in from the outside and do that unless they make a habit of doing it in their daily life."

Does Father Robert consider himself to be a teacher? I ask. He says he doesn't think it is his gift. "I may teach by example," the hermit tells me. "Like they say, you don't talk about life, you live it." Robert pauses, his dark eyes meeting mine in a direct glance. He exclaims, "You just do it!"

Still curious on the subject, I ask Father Robert if he has always thought in terms of teaching by living. "I never think in those terms!" He says it is the same with monastic life. "We are witnesses. But if we are sitting here because we are witnesses, then we are defeating our purpose." He tells me that a monk lives his life because he wants to love God. "If that gives witness, then well and good."

He can tell from my expression that I don't fully understand what he is saying. He leans toward me with his elbows propped on his knees and shares a simple story.

"When I came down from the hermitage one day I saw a flower, a beautiful flower. Now, nobody else may have seen that flower, but that doesn't make any difference. That flower was still giving glory to God by just being. And that is the same way I feel about my life. Nobody may see or know about me, but I am just giving glory to God."

We sit quietly for a moment until I nod my head to indicate that I understand. We stand and shake hands. "Peace be with you," he says.

"And also with you."

CHAPTER SIX

~

Holy Land

His *Rule* is written to help his followers scrutinize their
lives through the prism of scripture.

Verna A. Holyhead, SGS
The Gift of St. Benedict

Monastic economics is revolutionary,
calling for a conversion of materialism,
consumerism, and overconsumption—
so that no one is left outside the cosmic hospitality.

W. Paul Jones
Teaching the Dead Bird to Sing

*Wearing patched bib overalls, a white T-shirt, and a pair of high-top
work boots with worn soles, I meander through a vast wheat field,
where the stalks grow waist-high. A frayed straw hat covers my disheveled light brown hair and provides protection from the sun. In
the distance, the horizon looks as straight as a line drawn by a
draftsman dividing the indigo blue sky from the ocean of golden
wheat below.*

I hold a tiny baby wrapped in a soft, white cotton blanket close to my chest. His eyes are still closed, and he squirms in the shelter of my arms in search of a more comfortable spot. The baby is my son.

Because he is still in the formative stages of development, I can only communicate with him through gentle physical contact and bodily warmth. Verbal contact could be damaging to his health. We will get to know one another through the language of silence in this birthing process called "re-ignition."

For a few hours each day, I pick up my son and hold him carefully as we wander through the endless waves of wheat. The outing allows him to slowly acclimate to the fresh air and the sunshine. It is also a crucial time for bonding between father and son.

His name is Monkey Bonwit Gardenhouse III. Our community named him. It's our tradition: an aspect of the initiation ceremony into our world. The number designation is particularly appropriate. I was baptized Cornelius William Claassen II, after my paternal grandfather.

Because our time together is almost over, I turn around and walk back in the direction of a wire-and-wood-post fence that extends out in either direction as far as I can see. A soft, velvety pouch hangs from the fence. This is where Monkey will complete his incubation period. At the fence, I give him a gentle hug, place him back into the pouch, secure the snaps at the top, and back away. Tomorrow and every day thereafter I will return until my son is fully developed and able to go home with me.

On this sixth day of retreat I hunch over the desk writing with determination as the bell for Lauds begins to ring. I am mystified. It has been almost two decades since I had my first of many dreams about Monkey Bonwit Gardenhouse III.

My initial Monkey dream occurred while I was living in Israel, working as a laborer on Kibbutz Maabarot, an agricultural collective populated by over a hundred families. Located midway between Tel Aviv and Haifa, the kibbutz had been established years before in the former Palestine by European Jewish immigrants who identified as Democratic Socialists. On the kibbutz, labor responsibilities were shared by the adults and the children, with many of the jobs on a rotating schedule between the men and women. Its successful economy negated the use of money within the community. Couples were housed in comfortable apartments and, beyond infancy and early childhood, the young people lived in their own adult-supervised houses situated in a different area of the kibbutz. Each day the families would schedule several hours of "quality time" together with a focus on the children's needs.

At mealtimes, members and volunteers shared the tables in the community dining hall. And in the evening the coffee house became the recreation center, where we played games, socialized, attended concerts and films, and engaged in political discourse. The only television on the kibbutz, located in the meeting hall, was used for the nightly news and special public programming.

Kibbutz Maabarot provided a successful alternative to the dominant competitive and consumer-driven economy of the state. For me, it inspired a wealth of new ideas in education and labor relations, gender roles and parent-child relationships, as well as politics and the arts. Adults and children alike were encouraged to develop their talents. And the community was a leader in the Peace Now Movement, a political organization working to resolve the ongoing conflicts between the Israelis and the Palestinians.

I had purposely chosen to work on a secular kibbutz, where community members honored birthdays, agricultural holidays, and other special events based on the seasonal cycle. What better way to honor the Creator's generosity?

Throughout my Israeli stay, my dreams were frequent and always bigger than life. In my first encounter with Monkey, the setting was nearly identical to last night's dream: the indigo blue sky and the expansive wheat field were the same, but the fence was missing. In our first meeting, Monkey was a spirited, talkative, dark-skinned little boy with jet-black hair and Asian features. He looked as though the barber had placed a bowl on his head and cut around it. I remember galloping through the wheat field with Monkey bouncing along on my shoulders, laughing wildly. For a decade after our initial encounter he would intermittently revisit me in that recurring dream. Then the visits stopped. Now, Monkey has come back into my life. But this time he has returned as an infant.

I am hungry for more than food at the breakfast table. I want to share the dream and talk about my experiences on the Israeli kibbutz. But it seems so silly in the present scheme of things. Instead, I sit in silence and ponder how the dream relates to my life in this moment. Why has Monkey come back? Who or what does he symbolize? Why has he returned as a baby?

The word *war* catches my attention and abruptly pulls me into the conversation at the table. "I grew up in Munich, Germany, during World War II and was raised in a Benedictine monastery," reveals Hans. The Arkansas businessman's origins explain his slight accent. This morning he is relaxed, sitting at the table in jeans, long-sleeved sports shirt, and running shoes, sipping black coffee as he shares snippets of personal history. "It was a very oppressive atmosphere that had a profound effect upon me," he says. Hans is no longer a practicing Catholic. He believes that the teaching of original sin by the church effected the way the orphans were treated in the monastery. "We were always assumed to be guilty until proven innocent," he remarks caustically.

George Fox, the founder of Quakerism and a practicing Christian in seventeenth-century England, comes to mind as I listen to Hans talk. Fox taught something quite different. He did not accept the notion of original sin. "Fox believed that the divine spark within all people guides them toward the good, toward the best in themselves—toward God," writes Robert Lawrence Smith in *A Quaker Book of Wisdom*. "Therefore, all people carry within them the potential for perfectibility" (p. 5). Fox's vision was one of hope and trust that God will find expression within each of our lives. His vision was one of "original blessing."

"There's a way of looking at things as the glass is either half full or half empty," declares Hans. He thinks that the church dwells more on the half empty than the half full, and that presents a problem for him. "In that way of thinking, there's no joy in the good things of life," he says.

His friend, James, carries the discussion even further. He comments that the concept of original sin has been interpreted in such a way as "to oppress women for thousands of years." No one at the table disagrees. "The men who established church doctrine were simply trying to assuage their guilt," says James. "In so doing, a philosophy—an oppressive philosophy—was formulated."

"Are you expressing the viewpoints of your seminary professors?" asks someone. James makes it clear that his opinion is still not the majority viewpoint. He intrigues me—a onetime entrepreneur and capitalist role model who is now the seminary rebel.

Our conversation shifts from church dogma to the symbolic significance of Christ's representation on the cross: the crucified Christ versus the risen Christ. "In Latin America, the church historically presented the crucified Christ to the laity," I offer. "The pre–Vatican II church leadership in Central and South America was frequently aligned with the ultraconservative political forces and military leaders, not with the parish masses."

Another guest at the table comments that the crucified Christ was an influential symbol projected by the church to keep the masses passive and tractable. It strongly conveyed the idea that one must bear life's burdens rather than rise up and demand something better; life in the hereafter would be the reward for accepting one's lot on earth.

"I began to think about the difference between the risen and the crucified Christ when I traveled to Nicaragua in the mid-1980s with Witness for Peace," I share with the others. I was among a delegation of U.S. citizens who traveled to Nicaragua to witness the military conflict between the Sandinista government and the Contra forces, then covertly supported by the Reagan administration. I saw a disturbing view of the disastrous influence American foreign policy can have on another culture.

I remark that under the Sandinista government there evolved grassroots faith communities, the popular church. They reinterpreted biblical teachings, forging a new theology of hope and liberation. In those communities, the risen Christ was a symbol of hope in this lifetime.

Our breakfast discussions provide an opportunity for each of us to share our experiences and ideas and to raise questions about issues in our lives. As much as I seek out silence and solitude, I also wish to participate in these conversations. I benefit as much from the spoken words as I do from the collective silence—a new discovery.

Prior to midday prayer, I find the copy of the Latin psalter kept in the guest parlor. This bulky, thick volume, with large print and an illuminated, medieval-looking text, is the foundation of the liturgical hours. I close my eyes, finger through the pages, stop, and point to an unseen psalm. My finger lands on Psalm 101, verse 1. An English translation in a nearby Bible reads, "I will sing of mercy and justice; to You, O Lord, I will sing praises." This scripture will be my silent mantra in the coming service.

Nicaraguan Ernesto Cardenal—a novice under Thomas Merton's supervision, priest, internationally recognized poet, and former Sandinista cultural minister—comments in his book *To Live Is to Love* that "all the laws of nature are like the strings of a Psalter. The chant of the monks and the cycle of the liturgical year are in accord with the cycle of the harvest, the seasons of the year and the cycle of life and death." He goes on, "And thus the chanting of the monks in choir is a participation of the human soul in the rhythms of the sea, of the moons, and the reproduction of animals and stars" (p. 150).

Sitting next to Elizabeth in the sanctuary, I sense an unspoken bond with her, a feeling that I frequently experience with others in a silent Quaker meeting. Silently, I repeat the first verse of Psalm 101, while Elizabeth chants the scriptures with the monks.

During lunch I discover that Michael has left for Kentucky, and I notice that Steve has chosen to sit in silence at one end of the extended table. Again, I mention to my fellow guests that I am planning to write about this retreat experience, and that is why I frequently carry a camera and always take notes. I say it as much to alleviate my own discomfort as I do to make sure that all visitors are clear about my intentions.

"How is it going?" asks Frank.

Although the project is still in the formative stages, I answer as best I can. "It is going well. My project will focus on the community as a whole; monks, guests, and the author," I reply. "After experiencing dozens of retreats, I have come to appreciate that we are all part of the monastic community in this moment. That's what I hope to convey with my writing." As we eat I mention Henri J. M. Nouwen's *Genesee Diary* to Frank. It is an account of a lengthy stay at the Trappist monastery in upstate

New York where Frank made his first retreat. He is not familiar with the book.

"I have been surprised at how many feelings Nouwen and I have had in common," I tell the carpenter. "It may simply be a comment on what many people experience when they go on retreat despite the amount of time they spend there."

"Have you read Frank Bianco's *Voices of Silence?*" asks Pastor John.

"Yes, I found his spiritual journey fascinating," I answer. "He writes like an investigative journalist."

When one of the guests mentions the topic of mentors and heroes, I get up, clear my dishes, wash them, and exit the building for a walk down the gravel drive. The temperature has dropped, and a heavy snow is falling.

Mentors and heroes are revealing subjects for a retreat discussion. My list is endless: from religious figures, artists, and schoolteachers, to writers, mythologists, and vagabonds. It is difficult to imagine life without them. These individuals, living and dead, have provided me with a foundation and given me the strength to maintain a sense of self.

"Well, I'm finally caught up," declares Father Richard, looking up from the familiar hardbound ledger as I enter the dining room after my walk, brushing snow from the top of my head. His projects and responsibilities seem endless. "I had just a few more entries to put into the book."

Making myself a cup of tea, I envision Peter Beard's colorful and mysterious hardbound ledger scrapbooks, sections of which have been reproduced in books and magazines. Author, environmentalist, and commercial photographer, Beard updates his scrapbooks daily when residing at his rustic ranch near Nairobi, Kenya. Each overwhelming page in his seemingly endless number of volumes is an intriguing collage of the commonplace and the bizarre. It is a Rorschach test of Beard's state of mind in the moment. Pasted onto the pages are newspaper articles and random headlines intermixed with side notes, primitive illustrations, and sometimes handprints and footprints. One might find wads of gum, broken teeth, and good-luck charms pasted onto attached grainy but extraordinary-looking black-and-white wildlife photographs.

"I have been recording general events," explains Father Richard just as I am about to ask. He reads an entry about a senior monk fainting and being taken to a local hospital: a walk back in monastic time. Richard fingers past a few more pages to reveal an account of a community member flying to the East Coast to visit Benedictine monasteries. The unwieldy volume is a family tree presented in words instead of diagrams, a record of men who chose to die in one world only to be reborn into another. Richard's final recitation mentions gun blasts during hunting season that sound as if they are coming from the monastery's property.

"We didn't keep a journal the first eight years of our community," he confesses. "So, there is some confusion about events from that time period." He looks up at me through his thick glasses. "Recently, we even have had some confusion as to the original founding members."

Abruptly, Abbot Cyprian appears at the door dressed in jeans, a faded red hooded sweatshirt, and muddy work boots. Although he is clearly upset, he remains calm. "Half of the fruitcake orders were set in the tins upside down," he announces. "We are going to have to turn them over before the syrup dries. That's what the telephone call was about." He is talking about thousands of fruitcakes, and additional work demands on a community that is already stretched thin. This is a serious concern because fruitcake sales provide the abbey's primary income.

"Well, why didn't he say so when he talked to me?" Richard responds curtly without mentioning the man's name. Trying to smooth things over, Cyprian says that it was just a lack of communication, and they would all work it out. "Well, we have been trying to work it out for a long time," replies Richard in a cool tone.

Out of breath, Father Theodore rushes into the room dressed in work clothes. He says that he will cover the phone for the next half hour assuming Father Richard has more book entries to make. Monks face daily conflicts just like everyone else. That is part of living in community.

I plan to skip supper, but I spot a new arrival and decide to introduce myself before making a peanut-butter-and-jelly sandwich to take to my room. I need to catch up on some writing. Earlier in the afternoon I had seen him pacing the sidewalk outside the guest quarters with cigarette in hand.

"My name is Bill," he says, remaining in his chair and extending his hand to shake mine. His smoky, deep voice would play well on the radio. "I'm from the southwestern part of the state." Tall and stocky with broad shoulders, Bill wears a rumpled dark suit and a shirt with an open collar. His ancestry could be Native American. The new guest mentions that he has made many visits to the monastery over the last half-dozen years, and on one occasion he experienced a mystical visitation. I'm not surprised to hear this. Other guests have made similar comments in the past. I often think of my dreams as mystical visitations. "I have been here twenty times," Bill says, as I turn to go make my sandwich. "And I am back again to take care of some more business."

Before going to bed, I return to the dining hall for a late-night snack and find Frank reading intently in one corner of the room. He has been keeping a low profile. "Join me," he whispers. "I'm ready for a break, heh." He tells me how pleased he is to be back in a Trappist monastery years after his first retreat. "It's been a long thinking process for me."

I tell him that my first retreat was years ago as well. "There was a longing for the quiet and the solitude," I tell Frank, "but at my first retreat I was more interested in the community dynamics and the economics than the religion." The monastery was a self-sustaining community that offered an alternative vision of how people could live and work and worship together in a spirit of cooperation. "It was only after a number of monastic visits that I became more interested in the spiritual foundation of Trappist monasticism."

"Did you ever seriously consider becoming a Trappist yourself?" the carpenter asks.

"Briefly," I reply.

Frank is convinced that he will return to a Trappist monastery as a postulant after this introductory period—if not at Assumption Abbey, then possibly at the community up in Utah. But first he needs to take care of his affairs in Canada. "Among other things, I have to receive the church papers recognizing the annulment of my marriage and then obtain a list of legal papers from the state." Frank reveals that he has spent a lot of time these past few days reviewing his life. Tomorrow he begins a series of interviews with monks. His first meeting will be with Abbot Cyprian.

Frank's evaluation and review could involve at least a few more visits. The abbot and his fellow monks will want to be clear as to why he feels called to this life and what he expects from the community. If at the end of this process the monks decide to invite him back, Frank, like every other candidate, will be required to undergo a thorough psychiatric examination. In *The Province beyond the River: The Diary of a Protestant at a Trappist Monastery*, W. Paul Jones writes that "this strenuous life of the spirit is only for the strong, and it is better at the beginning that one understands this, and enters not as an escape or compensation, but as a call. . . . [The monks] are clear that the original desert fathers and mothers went to the wilderness not to escape, but to do battle—the desert is the citadel of the demons" (p. 30).

Every Time I Feel the Spirit

Every time I feel the Spirit
Movin' in my heart I will pray,
Every time I feel the Spirit
Movin' in my heart I will pray.

Up on the mountain, when my Lord spoke,
Out of His mouth came fire and smoke.
Looked all around me, it looked so fine,
Till I asked my Lord, if it were mine.

Every time I feel the Spirit
Movin' in my heart I will pray,
Every time I feel the Spirit
Movin' in my heart I will pray.

Oh I have sorrows and I have woe,
And I have heartaches here below.
But my God leads me, I'm in His care,
And I can feel Him everywhere.

Every time I feel the Spirit
Movin' in my heart I will pray,
Every time I feel the Spirit
Movin' in my heart I will pray.

∽ **Reflection** ∽

[The cellarer] should consider the pots of the monastery and all its goods as if they were the holy bowls of the altar. He must not hold anything as negligible. Let him not be controlled by avarice, nor should he waste or dissipate the goods of the monastery.

[The cellarer] should be a wise person, of mature character and well disciplined. He should not be gluttonous, arrogant, stingy, or wasteful.

St. Benedict
The Rule

Father Theodore

Called the "resident business tycoon" by the national media and "soft-spoken but enterprising" by a local newspaper journalist, Father Theodore has been the longtime business manager (cellarer) at Assumption Abbey. He, along with two assistants, oversees the community's fruitcake business and lumber and incense sales. In addition, they are responsible for the financial aspects of the monastery's guest wing.

Theodore also has a keen sense of humor. "I have a pen on my desk," he told one journalist, "and it says, 'Get even, give fruitcakes.'" In a *48 Hours* television segment titled "An Enduring Tradition" and featuring the monastery's fruitcake business, the narrator jokingly asks Father Theodore a question. "Now, I would be remiss in my duty, Father, if I didn't ask you if there were any similarity in the way you made concrete blocks and the way you make fruitcakes." Without missing a beat, Theodore responds, "There is no comparison, though fruitcakes and blocks both get better with age. But the fruitcakes remain moist and soft and edible, whereas the blocks get harder all the time" (CBS, December 23, 1992).

Theodore acquired his business acumen as an office manager for an auto finance company, where he worked just prior to entering the New Melleray Abbey at the age of twenty-five. "We would buy contracts on the automobiles from the dealer," he explains. "We had to exercise a lot of judgment. It gave me insight as to how to run an office to some extent."

Father Theodore was the first abbey member I met. He has always been friendly and hospitable. I pull up my chair next to his desk as he continues to sort through a stack of papers next to the in/out box.

Prior to this conversation, I had assumed that Theodore managed all of the major business endeavors at the abbey, but that is not the case. He explains that his work has been primarily with the concrete-block factory and the fruitcake business. "I wasn't heavily involved in the farm other than assigning work," he tells me. "I didn't have anything to do with managing it." Back in the early years there were individual managers for the farm, the vineyards, and the peach orchard. Theodore says that business management was finally consolidated with the advent of the concrete-block factory.

As Brother Boniface explained to me a few days ago, the transition from farming to the block factory began in the early 1960s. "The farm wasn't supporting us, and we had a creek full of sand and gravel," says the gray-haired monk, scratching his beard. Theodore explains that a Canadian monastery had a small block plant that was used as a prototype for the one in Missouri. "We originally envisioned it supplementing the farm work," he says. "A couple of brothers would make the blocks and sell them to the neighbors. But then the farm kept getting worse." Theodore blames its failure on fluctuating prices and poor management. "This really isn't farm country," Father Theodore explains. "It's primarily hay and pastureland. Our pastureland is about four hundred acres."

Father Theodore

The block plant took a long time to develop, according to Theodore. And the monks were responsible for building it. First they had to reroute the road, and then the community's ancient block machine had to be traded in for a newer model. "The old one was producing blocks that weren't square," he says with a smile, shaking his head.

At the point of investing in a new machine, the community had to decide if it was going to go bigger with the business and purchase a better machine, or try something else. He says that the abbot's advisory council voted in favor of buying a new machine and expanding the business.

"They (monasteries) are communistic communities where property is shared, with the time freed by collective labor given to contemplation and prayer," writes Fenton Johnson in *Keeping Faith*. "They are to be exemplars of life lived not for the future but in the here and now, a life built on and lived by faith" (p. 43).

By now, Theodore has set his papers aside. He pushes his chair away from the desk and begins to talk to me like a fellow businessman. "We hit a perfect market in the mid-1960s because everything was expanding," he says. "In the late 1960s and early 1970s, we could sell everything that we made. Our market was usually within seventy-five miles."

However, the block factory was labor-intensive and put tremendous physical demands on the aging community. I recall Brother Boniface's comment about some of the men getting older, although the list didn't happen to include him.

Theodore reveals that the truck drivers, the mechanics, and the plant manager were usually hired from the neighboring communities. "When the plant manager quit, we decided to take our losses and get out." He pauses for a minute, grabs a paper from the in/out box, gives it a quick glance and throws it back. "One of the employees wanted to buy it, so we sold it to him for a very attractive price. Then we had nothing for one and a half years."

The community remained solvent during that time. It had to. "Once we were made an abbey, in 1957, we were on our own," he explains. If the monks hadn't discovered a lucrative cottage industry, the monastery would have closed down.

Just a few weeks ago I attended a discussion group with the *Intentional Communities Directory* editor, and I mention it to Theodore. The directory, a commercial publication that can be ordered through most bookstores, is a compilation of more than 350 communal and collective communities scattered throughout the United States with economic arrangements similar to those of the monastery. I tell Theodore that some of these other communities are faith-based, while the majority of them are secular. But they all seek to create an alternative economic model in order to build communities that are cooperative in nature.

Theodore is surprised to hear about the directory. I explain that many of the cooperatives have created cottage industries, like the fruitcake business. And others have combined outside incomes with a homegrown business with the goal of becoming financially independent.

"Why did your community decide to develop a fruitcake business?"

"Because other Trappist communities had made fruitcakes, and some of our members were familiar with how to make them."

The resident business tycoon tells me that during the first year of fruitcake production they made close to eight thousand cakes and sold 75 percent of them. "That first year we advertised in eighteen different Catholic newspapers," he says, checking his watch. "Just by accident we were interviewed for a segment on the *MacNeil-Lehrer News Hour*, and we were also the subject of a feature article in the *Kansas City Star*."

The local and national publicity has had a tremendous impact on the fruitcake business. The St. Louis area, the abbey's largest market, has continued to grow. And Williams-Sonoma gourmet stores around the country continue to sell the fruitcakes and advertise them in their holiday gift catalog. "We made eighteen thousand cakes this year and sold out by mid-December," Father Theodore says with a satisfied grin.

At this point, all of the business functions are fully computerized. When I ask if the community can expand the fruitcake business at will, I can feel that Theodore is ready to wrap up our conversation. "To a certain extent, but it depends on how much advertising and PR we do," he replies. But given the size of the community, Theodore says that the operation can't expand much beyond the number of sales of this past year.

As I get up to leave, Father Theodore has one more thing he wants to share with me. "You know, it's just amazing that when you do what you can, it is providence," he says. "People call it luck. But it's really just coming along and picking up the pieces and making up for our mistakes."

His closing comment reminds me of a story that author Verna A. Holyhead, SGS, shares in *The Gift of Saint Benedict*. She writes that a monk once asked what he and his community did all day long. He replied, "We go on and fall down and get up, and go on and fall down and get up" (p. 20).

CHAPTER SEVEN

~

Women in the House

[T]he Hebrew word for God's Spirit, Ruach, is both mas-
culine and feminine, and thus emphasizes that God is
male and female.

Henri J. M. Nouwen
The Genesee Diary

We die and are reborn so many times. The passage from
one state of being to another occurs not just at birth and
death, but over and over throughout life.

Peter Matthiessen
quoted in *The Circle of Life* (David Cohen)

"'Jesus, Mary and Joseph,' I said to myself each time the car
slipped into the ditch and stalled," exclaims Brother Dominic to
the guests crowding around him at the breakfast table. He is the
center of attention. Yesterday, late in the afternoon, Dominic
drove into the nearby town for supplies during the snowstorm.
Because he didn't have chains, and the car was not a four-wheel
drive, it slid off the road and into the ditch four times.

Brother Dominic laughs as he tells his story with exaggerated facial expressions and sweeping gestures. "At one point I was waiting in a Pentecostal church. It was warm, you know, and I could use the restroom there." He shrugs his shoulders with a look of innocence. He must have been at Holiness Temple, where I had stopped a week ago only to find it closed. "Imagine me in a Pentecostal church," he says, rolling his eyes. He is a talented storyteller, who revels in sharing the minute details.

After the car slid off the road for the fourth time, Dominic gave up. "I wasn't going to stay in the car all night because I couldn't keep the engine running," he comments. "Well, I had seen a trailer home a mile or two back, so I got out of the car and started walking." A fellow who had helped him out of the ditch earlier drove by and offered him a ride back to the monastery. Dominic talks as though he had been halfway around the world, stranded, and then rescued. For a cloistered monk, his predicament must indeed have felt like a foreign experience.

While finishing breakfast, I give Frank a copy of *Genesee Diary* by Nouwen, the book I had recommended to him yesterday. Last night, after our conversation, I returned to the library and discovered it in a bookshelf. He beams with delight and begins to leaf through the book. "Reading about Nouwen's experiences will be like going back through a part of my life history," Frank says.

Breakfast talk is light—distinctly different from yesterday. Steve is again at the end of the table trying to maintain silence, but two new guests are putting him to the test. They are St. Vincent de Paul sisters who arrived last night. Their gray habits and traditional caps are a distinct contrast to the colorful pantsuit worn by Sister Elizabeth.

"We are looking for used computers, IBM or Macintosh, for a program of ours," says one of the sisters to long-haired Steve. "Can you give us some ideas as to how to find some?" He had mentioned earlier that he had worked part-time in a computer assembly plant. Steve shrinks back into his chair when she poses the question. "Well, I really don't know that much about them," he says quietly. Elizabeth, Hans, and James speak up and offer some ideas. Steve, visibly relieved, excuses himself from the table with dishes in hand.

My morning walk out the driveway and down the county road is invigorating. The air is blustery and bracing. Snow crunches beneath my boots and continues to fall in big icy flakes. Above me hundreds, perhaps thousands, of birds gather in swarms like mosquitoes and move from tree to tree making a deafening sound. They must be trying to stay warm and rummage for food as the temperature continues to drop.

While tramping along the partially plowed road, I think about the "wish for peace" at Mass this morning, when I made a special effort to shake hands with a senior brother. His ashen face, sunken eyes, and stoop-shouldered walk indicated that he was not well. One of the other monks had confirmed earlier that this brother was recovering from a serious illness. I wanted to share my strength and good health with a caring handshake and embrace. Instead, when I reached out and clasped his hand, it was his vibrant life energy that moved through me. His smile was engaging and his hands warm and hospitable.

I felt silly and naïve because of my assumptions. Our encounter was humbling. "'Let them strive to be the first to honor one another.' They should bear each other's weaknesses of both body and character with the utmost patience," (p. 57) wrote St. Benedict.

Following the Eucharist at this morning's Mass, I returned to the pew, shut my eyes, and drifted back in time to a profound event in my life. I am still puzzled as to why it surfaced then.

I was standing at a funeral in Arlington Cemetery on a muggy spring day. Beside me were my friends James and David

Snow cover on day seven

and James's other close friend Charlie. In front of us, standing at attention, were uniformed soldiers carrying rifles. Next to them was the official mourner provided by the army, who held a flag in her upturned hands.

James's estranged father, a World War II veteran, had recently died, been cremated, and was now scheduled to be entombed in the cemetery wall. Although James was a veteran who had served in Vietnam during the late 1960s, the rest of us had not been in the armed forces. Instead, we had all been active in the peace movement.

The four of us stood quietly at the ceremony site, looking straight ahead into the thousands of white crosses planted on the rolling, manicured grounds, as James read a few paragraphs that he had written in memory of his father. When he finished, there was a moment of silence, and the rifle salute commenced (three rifles firing simultaneously three times).

"Bang!" After the first rifle shots shattered the silence, I noticed a break in the horizon directly in front of me. It extended out on either side from where we were standing. Through the break, I could see thousands of men in the distance. My heart beat hard against my chest. "Bang!" They were men of all races, sizes, and nationalities. The men were marching together, not in uniform but in civilian clothes. I intuitively understood that they were from the past, the present, and the future. "Bang!" In that moment, the vision was clear. I was an integral part of all men who had lived before me; I was related to all men living today; and I was an ancestor of all men who would come into the world after my death. The break in the horizon snapped shut.

"All the communions of a lifetime are one communion," writes Pierre Teilhard de Chardin in *The Divine Milieu: An Essay on the Interior Life*. "All communions of all men now living are one communion. All the communions of all men, present, past and future, are one communion" (p. 102).

When I reawaken to the present, I am standing almost a mile down the county road near the snow-covered shell of the old monastery. Blanketed and partially hidden under the white cover, the ruins have become a part of the natural landscape. Turning around, I retrace my steps to the abbey.

Each retreat day I peel back yet another layer of consciousness and, in so doing, reach a deeper level of awareness and vulnerability. I continue to remove cultural and societal armor that I wear in the outside world. "People are stimulated and nourished when they come into this medium," says Snowmass Abbey's Dom Alexander in *Voices of Silence: Lives of the Trappists Today*. "When they muster the courage to stretch into what is very different here from their usual environment, they grow" (Bianco, p. 207).

Visiting the guest library before lunch, I comb the shelves in search of additional historical information about the abbey and discover photo albums. Organized in chronological order, the images begin with the early 1950s and continue through the next thirty years. It is one thing to read and hear about monastic history and quite another to actually see photographs of the men building their future. "I had to get my camera to register the things that were more important than how poor they were— their pride, their strength, their spirit," proclaimed the noted Depression-era photographer Dorothea Lange in Elizabeth Partridge's book *Restless Spirit: The Work and Life of Dorothea Lange* (p. 47). I discover the essence of Lange's comment as I review the images before me.

Black-and-white and often faded, the pictures reveal a farm cooperative and demanding physical labor. Monks are captured on film working in the vineyards, constructing wooden additions onto the old monastery, and repairing the once-famous swinging bridge, which has since been dismantled for safety reasons.

Members of the "elite strike force in the spiritual life," as author Frank Bianco called them, can be seen selectively logging and clearing the expansive acreage given to them by the Missouri businessman. Still other photographs show the brothers herding sheep and feeding cattle or straining to stack the finished product at their once lucrative concrete-block factory.

These flashes of monastic history divulge a rigorous and demanding spiritual boot camp, where the commitment was not for a mere six weeks but for a lifetime. It was a community where most of the men had already taken the sacred vows of stability, conversion of manners (chastity and poverty), and obedience.

Additional photographs broaden the scope of monastic life by capturing family visitations. At one time, family contact was limited to brief once-a-year visits at the monastery. Today's rules are less restrictive, taking into account the needs of individuals. Ceremonies and religious celebrations are also included in the albums. One extraordinary scene reveals the medieval ritual of a monk taking final vows: he lies prone on the sanctuary floor before the altar surrounded by his brothers.

"Immediately after the novice has placed on the altar a copy of his promises written in his own hand, he sings verse 116 of Psalm 119: 'Receive me, Lord, according to your promise and I will live. Do not disappoint me in my hope,'" explains Verna A. Holyhead, SGS, in *The Gift of St. Benedict.* "Three times this is sung, and three times the community repeats it, the last time adding the 'Glory be' in praise of the Trinity, the icon of every community." Holyhead says that the brother will then prostrate himself at the feet of each member of the community. "Symbolically, he throws himself on the mercy of God present in each of his brothers" (p. 56).

Many of the faces are unfamiliar. I know that some men returned to the motherhouse in Iowa. Others have died, and some have left the order, responding to a different call. I suspect that a few men have been asked to make another vocational choice. "If a brother is found to be stubborn or disobedient or proud, if he grumbles or in any way despises the holy rule and defies the orders of his seniors, he should be warned twice privately by the seniors in accord with our Lord's injunction (Matt. 18:15–16)," said St. Benedict. "If he does not amend, he must be rebuked publicly in the presence of everyone. But if even then he does not reform, let him be excommunicated, provided that he understands the nature of this punishment" (p. 25).

As I pass through the visitors' parlor with photo albums under my arms, two women guests walk in the door, put down their bags, and greet Father Richard. Obviously familiar with the community, one of the women gives Richard a warm hug. "Well, do you have my bed ready?" she asks in a demanding yet playful tone of voice.

"The beds aren't ready yet," replies Father Richard, throwing up his hands, "so you will have to give me some help."

"I will help make the beds. But I won't clean the bathroom," his sparring partner snaps back, laughing. She turns to her travel companion and says, "Why, I remember the time that he chewed me out for not making the beds just right!"

Richard stands there stammering, seemingly without words in this friendly game of one-upmanship. But he recoups with a colorful Irish joke.

As they gather their things and begin to move down the hallway toward their rooms, one of the women introduces herself to me. "My name is Peggy, and my friend here is Kate," she says. Probably in her mid-sixties, she is dressed comfortably in a cotton blouse and full skirt. Peggy's bobbed gray hair frames her round, friendly face. She reminds me of my high school English teacher. Kate, the quieter of the two, is a younger version of Peggy. She is wearing a sweater and slacks. They move on, following Richard down the hallway, and I slip into my room to clean up before lunch.

Fenton Johnson, in *Keeping Faith*, reveals that "monasticism and monastic time trace themselves not to the linear time of the later prophets and the Book of Revelation but to the round time that came before." He writes, "Monastic time is feminine time—the monastic space is essentially feminine space." He says that in Christian monasteries this may be more evident because of the predominant role of Mary, the Holy Mother. "As institutions dedicated to round feminine culture, monasteries give the priority to community over the individual" (p. 287).

In *The Monastic Impulse*, Walter Capps also addresses the relationship between the feminine and the contemplative. "A wise and perceptive prior told me once that the way to contemplative reality, at least for men, is through the discovery of the feminine side of their natures" (p. 18).

Elizabeth gets my attention in the dining room at lunchtime and motions for me to sit next to her. She has been quiet and solitary the last day or so. That often happens as guests sink deeper into their physical and psychological retreat time, so I am pleased to receive an invitation to join her. "I have been meaning to ask you why you decided to take on this particular writing project," she asks, sliding her chair away from the table so she can face me. "You could have written about so many other things that would have a broader appeal."

I sit down and think for a moment before answering. "At this time in my life, it is important to write on topics that I care about," I tell her. "Monastic life is a subject that has had a significant, no, a profound impact on my life, my spiritual development, and the way I relate to the world," I pause to take bites of baked chicken and rice. "For decades I have been making monastic retreats. They have been places of renewal for me, neutral territory where I have been able to rethink and reevaluate issues in my life." Elizabeth nods knowingly. "I want to share some of these experiences. So I am doing it with the pen and the camera." I explain that this retreat, in particular, has been a rewarding experience because of the strong sense of community among the guests and the monks.

Elizabeth says that my attempt to relate to other guests is an admirable quality. She pats me on the back as if to say "good for you." And yet, she also honors the importance of leaning into the silence and the solitude.

Hans, James, and Steve have decided to leave after lunch because of the current weather conditions and the forbidding forecast. The guest roster continues to change.

A brother reads Matthew 5:37 at Vespers. As a Quaker would say, it speaks to my condition. "If you mean yes, then say yes," he recites from the podium. "If you mean no, say no. All else between is created by the devil."

For me, the message is profound. I sit in the darkness and consider how often I have used the word *maybe* to avoid making a commitment or to delay making a decision on a weighty subject. It is a devilishly bad habit that creates turmoil in my life. I remain in the sanctuary after everyone else leaves and repeat the words over slowly and quietly—"If I mean yes, say yes. If I mean no, say no. All else is created by the devil." I will carry this mantra with me out of the monastery.

In the buffet line I am told that the St. Vincent de Paul sisters and Bill also decided to leave early because of the snow. During the quiet meal, Peggy interrupts the silence briefly and tells us that she makes church vestments as one means of bringing in an income. A short time later, Kate reveals that she is studying for her master's degree in psychoanalysis at a private institute in her hometown. Then silence returns to the dining hall. We are a reflective group this evening. As we finish the meal and sit quietly with our hot drinks, Dominic shuffles in to stack the clean dishes and remove the hotplates

Guest Peggy

and the leftovers. I think he wants us to start clearing the table.

"You know how many feminists it takes to screw in a light bulb?" he blurts out, breaking the silence, as he takes a stand at one end of the table. He grins and waits for a reply.

"Uh-oh," says Peggy, rolling her eyes. "I don't think I want to hear this."

Brother Dominic stands there a moment longer, letting the suspense build. He dramatically draws in a deep breath and answers, "You are not supposed to ask that question." That is the punch line. Moans fill the dining room and drive Dominic back into the kitchen. He has succeeded; we clear our plates and share clean-up duties.

Sitting at my desk a few hours later, I reread a section in *Genesee Diary*. Frank has let me borrow the book until tomorrow morning. Like Johnson and Capps, Nouwen also addresses the significance of the feminine in monastic life: "The feast of Our Lady's Assumption is an important feast for monks because under this title Mary is the patroness of all the monks." Nouwen spent many months at the Genesee Abbey in upstate New York. "I didn't understand this well enough when I came here, but the longer I am here, the more I realize that Mary is for the monks the most pure contemplative" (p. 90).

Oh Freedom

Oh freedom, oh freedom
Oh freedom over me!
And before I'd be a slave, I'd be buried in my grave,
And go home to my Lord and be free.

No more fear, no more fear,
No more fear over me!
And before I'd be a slave, I'd be buried in my grave,
And go home to my Lord and be free.

There'll be singing, there'll be singing,
There'll be singing over me.
And before I'd be a slave, I'd be buried in my grave,
And go home to my Lord and be free.

~

CHAPTER EIGHT

A Circle Unbroken

Do good and leave behind you a monument of virtue the
storms of time can never destroy.

Mennonite proverb
Wisdom of the Plain Folk

The thought manifests as the word;
The word manifests as the deed;
The deed develops into habit
And the habit hardens into character.
So watch the thought and its way with care,
And let it spring from love
Born out of concern for all beings.

The Buddha
as quoted in *Life Prayers from Around the World*
(Roberts and Amidon, 1996)

Out of bed and dressed before the bell begins to ring, I have
every intention of attending Vigils. In fact, I planned to go early
and meditate before anyone else arrived. But when I reach the
double doors leading into the sanctuary, I hesitate and listen to

a persistent inner voice that encourages me to consider an alternative. Heeding the call, I return to my room and pull on my boots and heavy coat, stocking cap, and gloves, then grab my flashlight, and make a beeline for the exit.

Outside in the frosty air, I kick through the snow with the flashlight beam leading the way. The early-morning darkness is welcoming. Like the Sirens of Titan, it lures me deeper into the unknown. Out here in this dense woodland is where I wish to honor the bigness of God. This morning I want to reach beyond the four walls of the sanctuary, beyond the words of the scriptures and the rhythms of the chants, and experience the hallelujah of creation.

Moving still farther into the darkness, I begin to experience a lack of physical sensation similar to that of floating in one of John C. Lilly's isolation tanks. It was something I used to do to achieve deep meditative states. The tank, developed in the latter half of the twentieth century, was a single-person sealed chamber, where I floated in saturated saline solution warmed to body temperature. There was neither light nor sound to intrude upon the experience. I continue to trek through nature's icy white powder, weaving in and out among the trees, until I reawaken to the reality of the numbing cold, turn around, and hurry back.

"What is essential in the monastic life is not embedded in buildings, is not embedded in clothing, is not necessarily embedded even in *The Rule*," said Thomas Merton in his last speech, presented at an international monastic conference near Bangkok. "It is concerned with this business of total inner transformation. All other things serve that end." Paul Wilkes captured it on film in his documentary titled "Merton: A Film Biography."

Back in my toasty room, the business of "total inner transformation" weighs on my mind as I sink into the overstuffed chair with a pen and a yellow legal pad in hand. A stream-of-consciousness flow of names, snippets of conversations, re-membered smells, colors and textures, and events from the past week pours out onto the lined pages. But these memories don't really address the issue of transformation. I feel stuck.

"Stuckness shouldn't be avoided," Robert Pirsig writes in *Zen and the Art of Motorcycle Maintenance*. "It's the psychic predecessor of all real understanding" (p. 286).

Trying another approach, I scrawl down questions that are nagging me. Have I spent enough time at the abbey, gathered enough impressions to be able to convey a sense of monastic life to a larger audience? Are my observations valid for anyone but me? Will my conversations and experiences provide insight into achieving the inner transformation of which Merton spoke?

I am distracted by hunger. Images of peanut butter and honey on Saltines beckon me into the darkened dining hall, where I hurriedly prepare a snack and then retreat to my room to eat and review my notes. But soon, warm and fed, I fall asleep sitting in the easy chair, wrapped in a cocoon of thermal blankets.

I am the first person in the refectory for breakfast, surprised and delighted by what I discover. Neatly arranged place settings and name cards, decorated in rich shades of red and pink, cover the extended table. In front of each name sits a homemade card and a candy heart. The bright morning sunlight streams through the bank of windows, highlighting the warm colors spread out over the table. Today is February 14—Valentine's Day!

"Good morning, Bill!" calls Brother Dominic as he carries a bowl brimming with apples and oranges from the kitchen to the buffet table.

"Morning, Dominic." I point to the table with a question-ing look. He grins and shrugs his shoulders as he returns to the kitchen. I find my place at the table, sit down, and read the card. Instead of serving myself breakfast, I remain seated. I am curious about the other guests' reactions.

"I can't remember the last time someone gave me a Valentine's card," Frank mumbles to himself when he discovers his place setting. He sits down and carefully opens his card, his lips moving as he silently reads the words to himself.

When Pastor John saunters into the room he stops abruptly, looks around at the decorations, and breaks into an ear-to-ear grin. He, too, delays breakfast and moves to the table in search of his name card and Valentine greeting.

The moment they enter the room, Peggy and Kate fall silent as they peruse the thoughtful arrangements. The two friends find their places and pick up their cards as though they were expensive pieces of crystal.

We know who is responsible for this grand gesture of kindness. And all of us pour out our feelings of gratitude when a coy-looking Elizabeth enters the room. She beams and acknowledges our expressions of delight. The abbey's welcoming environment seems to evoke generosity and kindness in all of us.

To our surprise, Elizabeth's mother, Mildred, arrives and joins us for breakfast. A gray-haired image of her daughter, Mildred is eighty-six, vivacious, and spirited; she interacts easily with the rest of us. Despite the snow, Elizabeth's aunt Dotty and uncle Ted have brought Mildred to visit for the day. They enter the dining room briefly, introduce themselves, and leave.

As we eat, Elizabeth mentions to her mother that I was in El Salvador during the recent civil war. Mildred has visited the country within this last year, as a member of a church group. "It was the most wonderful week of my life," she exclaims. "I mean it." Mildred shares her memories of traveling to rural communities and meeting with the children. She loved holding the very young ones. "I don't speak Spanish," Mildred admits, "but I was able to communicate with them in other ways." She mentions touch and facial expressions. "Did you go to El Salvador with an organization?" she asks me.

"No," I reply. "I went there to do some investigative work of my own and to visit friends working with a Catholic social justice group called the Cleveland Mission." Margaret nods her head knowingly. The Cleveland Mission, comprising priests and sisters and lay volunteers, has had a noticeable presence in El Salvador for many years. "The mission members were living in three different villages, one of which was in a combat zone," I comment. "They were brave and committed." I explain that the mission teams were frequently under surveillance by the Salvadoran military and the paramilitary forces that plagued that country.

"I was in the middle of San Salvador in October 1986 when the big earthquake hit," I continue. "It was devastating." I was planning to visit political prisoners held in a facility near the capital that morning. In the afternoon, I was scheduled to meet with a group of mothers whose sons and daughters had disappeared and were presumed to be dead, victims of right-wing death squads. Many of the missing were students who had been active in progressive politics.

"An hour before my prison visit, the quake hit the center of the city with tremendous force," I inform the others. "I was walking down the middle of a side street when buildings began to collapse, and screaming men and women emerged from the wreckage desperately seeking open areas." By the time I managed to get back to the mission group, the local villagers were organizing food assistance efforts.

"As you know, those villagers survive on a subsistence income," I say, looking over at Mildred. "But yet they made tortillas and cooked beans daily and managed to transport them into the city center for distribution." People who had practically nothing found a way to help their fellow citizens.

"Their faith is very strong," says Mildred. She mentions attending Mass at a few churches during her stay in El Salvador.

I, too, had an opportunity to worship with village parishes, known as "Christian base communities." Much like the "popular church" in Nicaragua, the base communities met regularly to reflect on issues of social justice, poverty, and repression. "The people do not use complicated words—most are barely literate—but as attested by priests and nuns who work with the communities, their observations are often profound because they live their theology through solidarity, charity and self sacrifice," explains Penny Lernoux in *People of God: The Struggle for World Catholicism*. "Theology is not an ivory-tower science but the practical application of faith, and as such it can challenge the secular and religious authorities on many issues, from agrarian reform to birth control and lay ministers" (p. 79).

I tell my tablemates that I continued to work on Central American issues while living in Washington, D.C. "During that time I and many others were arrested for participating in a nonviolent demonstration at the Pentagon," I comment. Thousands of activists concerned with the Salvadoran conflict converged on the Pentagon early in the morning to show our opposition to its continued military support of the repressive regime in that country. "Scores of us were arrested, booked, and given court dates, and then released later in the day." Mildred and the others at the table listen intently.

"I encountered many people, young and old, who were missing arms and legs because of the war," Mildred tells us. She understands.

I mention that it is ironic that a Republican president, Dwight D. Eisenhower, warned the American people that if we didn't maintain tight control over the military-industrial complex it would eventually maintain control over us. "In the councils of government, we must guard against the acquisition of unwarranted influence, whether sought or unsought, by the military-industrial complex," stated Eisenhower in his farewell address on January 17, 1961. "The potential for the disastrous rise of misplaced power exists and will persist." His warning was prescient.

Only when Brother Dominic sticks his head into the dining room and asks us to clear our dishes do we realize how long we have been talking. He reminds us that Sunday Mass will begin at 9:00.

I gladly offer to wash the dishes. With a towel in hand, Peggy joins me, and we continue to talk as I pass the wet dishes her way. Now that her children are grown, Peggy says that she is in a position to explore her life and organize her own schedule. "I write anywhere from three to six hours a day," she reveals. "I curl up on the end of the couch with a legal pad and a fine-point pen."

"I did that very thing early this morning," I tell her, "but I fell asleep before I got much work done." We agree that a designated writing environment and special writing tools are important in the creative process. "There are rituals connected to everything, even writing," I comment.

"A very wise priest told me once that we can know the will of God for our life in what we want and like to do," says Peggy. "So write, he told me!" She explains that she has successfully integrated monastic retreats, journal writing, and church activities into her new schedule. "I am just one monkess in the midst of many monks," she says sweetly as she dries a handful of silverware.

I grab another stack of dirty dishes from beside the sink and put them into the soapy water as Peggy comfortably leans her hip into the kitchen cabinet as if she were at home. "This is the very thing in which I am becoming more and more involved, just being," she admits. "But I am having difficulty because I have always been a doer." One of the monks, Brother Ben, has tried to tell her that she is "doing in simply being."

Brother Dominic returns to the kitchen and mentions that Mass will begin very soon. "You are going to be late to your own funerals," he jokes on his way out.

When we reach the sanctuary, it is filled with worshippers from the surrounding area, not unusual on a Sunday morning. Our extended retreat family has spread out among them on both sides of the room. As we sit down, I notice Elizabeth's aunt and uncle sitting in one of the front pews.

At every Mass, the presiding priest invites the congregation to offer prayers of intercession: petitions to God on behalf of the ailing and the lonely, the destitute and the victims. It is a somber and thoughtful, sometimes emotional, ritual when individuals remember loved ones and offer prayers and support for those in need. Some requests are very personal, while others are more general in nature. The prayers provide an opportunity for community members to lend support to one another. At the conclusion of each request, we repeat in unison, "Lord, hear our prayer."

It is unusual for me to make a request, but this morning I am moved to stand and ask that we pray for my younger sister. Recently she has had a particularly difficult time with the multiple sclerosis she's been struggling with for years. "Lord, hear our prayer," repeats the congregation, and I sit down.

Following several more requests, Elizabeth's uncle Ted rises from the front pew; he remains silent for a moment as if collecting his thoughts. Then he begins to speak slowly and forcefully. But Ted does not request prayers. He asks for God's condemnation of particular people and specific organizations; gay men and lesbians are at the top of his list.

Graphic passages from the Book of James (3:6–12) come to my mind as Ted rambles on. They were mentioned during a service earlier in the week, and I had taken the time to look them up. They speak to the power of the tongue.

"The tongue is such a flame. It exists among our members as a whole universe of malice," writes James. "The tongue defiles the entire body. Its flames encircle our course from birth, and its fire is kindled by hell. Every form of life, four footed or winged, crawling or swimming, can be tamed and has been tamed, by mankind; the tongue no man can tame. It is a restless evil, full of deadly poison." Christ's disciple continues, "We use it to say, 'Praised be the Lord and Father'; then we use it to curse men, though they are made in the likeness of God. Blessing and curse come out of the same mouth. This ought not be, my brothers!"

Ted's words swirl in my mind as he petitions the Creator to take his side and condemn the others. Looking over his way, I notice his wife, Dottie, huddling into the pew as though she is trying to disappear. When Ted finishes and sits down, there is a moment of uncomfortable silence before someone initiates the usual response, "Lord, hear our prayer." I say nothing.

As a gay man, I am deeply troubled by his comments. My ears burn, and my anger builds; it begins in my gut, moves into my chest, and finally crowds into my throat. I grab the pew in front of me, ready to stand. My unrehearsed response is desperate to be released. I know the power of the tongue because I, too, have used it as a weapon. "Stay cool," I say to myself silently. I take deep breaths, loosen my grip, and finally relax back into the pew.

During the Eucharist celebration, I seek relief and envision Elizabeth holding the chalice and carpenter Frank offering the host. I see the three of us creating a circle with the other parishioners and singing a rousing gospel song—a hand-clapping, foot-stomping kind of number. I quietly join the community, participate in the ritual, and return to the pew.

How ironic that Ted should come into the community on Valentine's Day, a day when people express love and kindness. Henri Nouwen, in his *Genesee Diary*, writes that "a monastery is not built to solve problems but to praise the Lord in the midst of them" (p. 194). This situation forces me to confront myself. What have I learned during my stay? Am I any closer to that inner transformation of which Merton speaks? Am I going to angrily confront Ted and use my tongue as a weapon?

After Mass, I don't linger in the sanctuary but move directly to the double doors and the nearby outdoor exit. The sunshine is blinding; it reflects off the snow covering everything in sight. I laugh at myself and think how easy it is to lose control and become entangled in the words of others.

As I stand in the grove of giant pine trees near the front of the sanctuary, I catch a glimpse of Dyers out of the corner of my eye. He is approaching me. I remain still, ignoring his presence. When I don't acknowledge him, he walks around and stands directly in front of me, looks up, and wags his tail. Against my better judgment, I lean over slowly and stroke his head and back in silence. And he accepts my show of affection. When I stop petting, Dyers shakes himself off, tramps away, and disappears around the corner of the monastery.

Ted and Dottie have asked to join the other guests for lunch and are already at the table when I enter the dining room. I sit directly across from them, introduce myself, and shake their hands. Dottie, a middle-aged woman with curly brown hair, looks weathered and uncomfortable. She sits dutifully and quietly by her husband's side. Ted, a dour-looking individual with slicked-back hair, doesn't say much. He appears more interested in eating than communicating.

I excuse myself to get a glass of water, and when I return to the table, I begin asking Dottie some questions. I want to engage her in conversation. Where are you from? Do you have a large family? How often do you visit the monastery? She seems surprised that someone is paying attention to her. Ted just keeps on eating. Dottie's expression becomes more open, and her posture improves as she talks briefly about her life. Among other things she reveals that her son, an only child, has recently taken temporary vows in a monastic order unfamiliar to me. I can't tell whether she is pleased or disappointed, sad or just resigned to her son's decision. Ted and Dottie finish their meals rather quickly and excuse themselves; they have scheduled a meeting with one of the monks.

Peggy and Kate, Frank and John, Elizabeth and her mother, and I linger at the table simply enjoying one another's company: humans being, not doing, or "doing by simply being," as Brother Ben would say. We only get up for cups of coffee or tea and more cookies. When one person speaks, the others listen with interest. No one mentions Ted's comments.

The four women do most of the talking this easy Sunday afternoon. Elizabeth and Mildred share stories about moving in together and the adjustments that they are going through. They sound more like best friends than mother and daughter. Mildred tells us that she is involved in social service projects in the community. She has recently been working at a local hospital, teaching new mothers how to breast-feed. Elizabeth admits that she has been feeling overwhelmed by the demands of her new job. And Peggy and Kate reminisce about their longtime friendship and life in their hometown.

They are the first to push away from the table, clear their dishes, and say their good-byes. Half an hour later Elizabeth and Mildred get up to leave. Their relatives have finished with their meeting and want to get on the road. "We sure would like to stay longer," says Elizabeth, "but we want to get back before dark."

I leave John and Frank to the dishwashing, fetch my coat and gloves, walk back outside, and begin to clear the front walks. It is the third time in two days. I welcome the exercise. Brother Stan, who is always quite reserved, drives by on the community bulldozer and waves. "Thanks for shoveling the walkways!" he yells. "It's a great help!"

Father Theodore is in a flurry of activity when I return inside. Dressed in his hooded sweatshirt and black jeans, he is packing canned goods and other food items into a cardboard box. An emergency food request was just called in. "Usually we get calls into the monastery for food requests," says Theodore, "although there are times when people come to the guest entrance and ask for assistance." The Trappists play a vital role in the surrounding community. Although they are officially a cloistered order, the monks necessarily have frequent contact with the outside world in order to survive and to fulfill St. Benedict's wishes.

Late in the afternoon, Frank, John, and I meet in the parlor as previously planned and exit through the guest door for a brief walk. We talk casually about religious practices in the United States as well as in Canada, a topic in which all three of us have various degrees of interest. I talk of my family's Mennonite history and my own familiarity with the Quaker tradition, commenting that both faiths are committed to pacifism and social justice. I mention my past contact with the Bruderhoffs, Christian communities in the United States that live collectively and commit themselves to social issues on a national and international scale. Their communities' economies function like those of monasteries: from each according to his ability, to each according to his need.

Pastor John is more familiar with the mainline Protestant denominations. He talks of his work with the United Methodist Church and infrequent contact with Southern Baptist congregations in Tennessee. Although John has been an ordained minister for years, he again expresses his interest in becoming an oblate of a monastic community.

"Why don't you just turn your world upside down and enter a monastery as a postulant?" I ask, only partly in jest.

"Because I enjoy sex too much," he responds, half jokingly. John feels a compelling call to a quieter, more thoughtful, spiritual life, and he is trying to figure out how to make that happen and still maintain his marriage and outside interests.

Winter solitude

Frank doesn't say much as we cut a trail through the snow on the partially cleared county road. He grew up in the Roman Catholic Church and that has been his primary faith community. What he does say is a reflection of his experiences in his hometown parish. He is obviously very much in the throes of a struggle about his future: is monastic life his true calling?

We sit together at Compline for the last time, the only guests in the sanctuary. I plan to leave in the morning before breakfast. Pastor John will depart later in the day and go visit his spiritual guide and friend in a nearby city. But Frank will stay a few days longer and meet with more of the monks to continue his discernment process.

Tonight, a trio of Father Theodore, Brother Benedict, and Father Richard sings a special selection in Latin. Their melodious voices blend beautifully. Yet another St. Valentine's Day gift to the community.

In this final liturgical hour of the day, the monks return to Psalm 4—"I will both lie down in peace, and sleep; for you alone, O Lord, make me dwell in safety." And also to Psalm 91—"He shall cover you with His feathers and under His wings you shall take refuge; His truth shall be your shield and buckler." These two scriptures "remind us that we all need protection from forces beyond our control, even as they reassure us that protection is ours," says Kathleen Norris in Cloister Walk. "The night will come with its great equalizers, sleep and death. It will pass over us, and bring us forth again into light" (p. 381).

We stand with the monks when they sing the Salve Regina, Mater Misericordiae to Mary, whose face is outlined by a single candle flame behind the altar. Our threesome falls into line behind the monks, and we move single file toward the abbot. Each of us bows and receives the sprinkle of holy water, leaves the sanctuary, and begins the "Great Silence."

Although tired when I return to my room, I feel compelled to make one final entry in my journal. What is it I want to cap-

ture on paper? Is it a quote from a guest or a scripture from one
of the services? Perhaps it is a comment from one of the
monks. I sit and wait for an inspiration; it soon comes to me. I
want to create a dream, the one that I would request, if asked,
on my final night at the monastery. It will include a full cast of
characters: monks and guests alike—the entire community.
And I begin to write.

*Monks and guests gather in a candlelit Gothic cathedral filled
with the smell of incense. At one end of the sanctuary is an enor-
mous rose window that spins through colors like a kaleidoscope in
the hands of a child. At the other end sit the dark ornate wooden
choir stalls and a smooth, circular black marble altar above which
hangs a simple wooden cross.*

*As the cathedral bells begin to ring, retreat guests and monks
alike enter through the side doors in the back and line up according
to gender. The monks, led by Abbot Cyprian, are wearing their
white hooded cowls, and the male guests are dressed in laymen's
clothes. Sister Elizabeth leads the female guests, who are wearing in-
formal attire. As the echo of the final bell fades away, our two lines
begin a meditative procession toward the front. At the altar steps,
our lines begin to intersect and form a circle around the black marble table; men and women alternate around the altar. And our celebration begins.*

*Abbot Cyprian initiates the "peace blessing," which moves
around the circle, each person greeting the next with a hug and a
handshake. Afterward the Lord's Prayer is led by Sister Elizabeth.
We don't speak the words: we chant them in unison—the men and
women alternating the lines. At the conclusion of the prayer, Elizabeth and Cyprian advance to the altar and lift the two small silver
host trays above their heads. "Through Him, with Him, and in
Him, in the unity of the Holy Spirit, all glory and honor is yours,
Almighty Father and Mother, forever and ever," we repeat together.
They return to the circle, break off pieces of the host, and pass the*

trays around. When the trays reach the opposite end of the circle, they are placed back on the altar.

Elizabeth and Cyprian once again move to the table, lift up the two silver chalices, and return to the circle. Each of them sips from the cup and then passes it to the next person. When the chalices reach the other side of the circle they, too, are placed back on the altar.

Our community joins hands, and one by one, each person repeats the phrase "Blessings and gratitude." We then drop hands, turn in the direction of the ever-changing, multicolored rose window, and begin slowly walking down the steps and into the aisle as the organist begins to play a bluesy rendition of the popular African American spiritual "He's Got the Whole World in His Hands." As our meditative walk transforms into a swinging motion down the aisle, we begin to clap to the rhythm of the beat, kick up our feet, and break out into song.

> He's got the whole world in his hands.
> He's got the big, wide world in his hands.
> He's got the whole world in his hands.
> He's got the whole world in his hands.

> She's got you and me, brother, in her hands.
> She's got you and me, sister, in her hands.
> She's got you and me, brother, in her hands.
> She's got the whole world in her hands.

The heavy bronze cathedral doors swing open, and we flow out into the darkness, dancing and clapping, stomping, and singing the final verse:

> He's got the sun and the moon in his hands.
> She's got the wind and the rain in her hands.
> He's got the sun and the moon in his hands.
> She's got the whole world in her hands.

Epilogue

I leave the engine running and trudge through the deep snow to the front porch of a Cape Cod–style house clustered with a half-dozen others in rural eastern Iowa. It is the only one with lights on inside. After rapping on the latched screen door, I hear mumbling coming from inside, and notice a man peeking out at me through a slit in the living room curtains. In a moment, the porch light flicks on, and the front door opens slightly.

"Hi, I am trying to find the New Melleray Abbey, but I am sure that I missed the turnoff. Can you give me directions?" I blurt out the string of words, hoping to convey a nonthreatening need. The door opens wider, revealing a short, heavyset man in a red plaid robe and slippers. A cigar hangs out of his mouth. "You have driven a few miles too far, fella," he says in a slow, easy manner. "What you want to do is drive back towards the main highway till you come to a blacktop road on your right. You'll see a small sign there for the monastery. Can't miss it."

I thank the man as he closes the door slowly; he leaves the porch light on until I make my way down the slippery steps and back to the car. A few miles down the road, I spot the unobtrusive sign through the heavy falling snow. The road is practically invisible.

At the end of the icy, snow-covered drive is a group of signs and arrows that point me to a parking lot in front of a stately three-story limestone building: the guesthouse. It's quite a contrast to the humble, concrete-block guest wing at Assumption Abbey. With backpack hanging from my right shoulder and book bag over my left, I plod up the steps, through the double doors, and into a tastefully designed foyer. A notice hangs on an office door to my right: "Be back at 7:50." Close by stands a finely crafted grandfather clock in a light-colored wood cabinet. Its pendulum steadily marks the minutes.

After putting down my baggage and peeling off my coat, I take a seat on the hallway bench and wearily lean back against the wall, exhausted. I've spent the day driving on treacherous roads through near-blizzard conditions. The foyer's beige walls and light brown carpeting and the hypnotic ticking of the clock are soothing.

"Oh, hello," says a monk who has just come around a corner into the hallway. Dressed in his white cowl, he reminds me of Brother Boniface. The man doesn't introduce himself. "I'm the night porter. Would you sign the register, please," he says in a formal tone. Boniface's image melts away. The night porter disappears briefly into the office. When he reemerges, I extend my right hand and introduce myself.

"My name is Father Tom," he responds hurriedly, with the obligatory handshake. "The official guest master will be here in the morning."

Tom assigns me to a room on the second floor. "We have enough space for thirty guests," he says as we climb the stairs. The building's interior looks recently remodeled; a faint but pleasant smell of fresh paint is in the air. As we reach the landing, he mentions the coffee and video room in the basement, points out the library down the hall, and leads me to my room at the other end of the corridor. "I can give you a key to the front entrance if you plan to go back outside tonight," says Tom, opening the door.

"Thank you. I would like that," I reply.

The monk briefly describes the layout of the monastery, hands me a daily schedule, and quietly excuses himself. It is a comfortable space with furnishings similar to those at Assumption Abbey. A wooden shelf with a dowel and empty hangers is mounted on the wall near the door of the bathroom. Two curtained windows look out onto the snow-covered grounds in front of the building. Strangely, the small room is devoid of religious symbols—no cross, no pictures of Mary or a smiling pope, and no Bible on the desk. It is oddly refreshing.

Sitting down on the firm twin bed and looking over the materials I was given, I notice that there are two guest schedules: one for group retreats and the other for individual self-guided stays. The monks' schedule is identical to that of Assumption Abbey.

Without unpacking, I grab my journal and pen, return to the first floor, and seek out the sanctuary. Although stark, it is striking in its beauty and its size. Two tiers of arched windows line one of the bare limestone walls. Originally they were covered with plaster "until the architectural consultant that the monks hired to help them remodel discovered that underneath the plaster were walls of native stone," explains Kathleen Norris in a *Poets & Writers Magazine* article written by Ray Kelleher. "The monks themselves did the work uncovering them, and now the church is a place where one can sit and wait and watch the play of sunlight and shadow, a place made holy by the simple glory of light on stone" (p. 64). Built into the opposite wall is a single tier of upper-level windows.

Above the altar, at the opposite end of the long sanctuary, are two large arched windows. The high, narrow ceiling is reinforced with dark wooden beams. Contemporary and undecorated choir stalls line the walls on either side of the aisle, emphasizing the sanctuary's mix of traditional Cistercian architecture and late-twentieth-century elements.

I sit down in one of the guest pews, which are separated from the rest of the interior by a simple wrought iron metal railing. Behind me, close to the door, is the heavy stone baptismal font. From the back pew I notice candle flames flickering close to the altar. Their shadows dance across the stone walls. Nearby, a man dressed in layman's clothes is kneeling up against a visitors' pew, holding his head between his hands.

After a brief meditation, I exit and walk outside, but the bitter cold quickly drives me back to the warmth of the guest quarters. Tired but hungry, I find my way down to the coffee and video room, and discover the old standbys: crackers and crunchy peanut butter. Cold orange juice in the fridge is a welcome addition to the snack.

While eating, I begin to rummage through the collection of inspirational videos on a shelf next to the VCR and discover a copy of *Merton: A Film Biography*. A friend has highly recommended it. I pull up a chair, turn on the VCR, and insert the video.

The documentary opens with a grainy black-and-white film clip of Merton speaking from a podium. Wearing his Trappist garb and black-framed glasses, he is addressing a group of men and women attending an international monastic conference near Bangkok in 1968. The clip was reportedly made just a few hours before his accidental death by electrocution. "Christianity is against alienation," he declares. "Christianity revolts against an alienated life."

The narrator reveals that Merton was "hailed as a prophet and condemned as a blasphemer." He was a "mystic and a poet" who couldn't escape the real world. He was a Western monk who forged a bond with the East, and the monastic conference in Thailand was an outgrowth of his efforts.

Through his writings, I have come to understand that Merton, or Father Louis as he was known at Kentucky's Abbey of Gethsemani, was keenly aware of the importance of bringing together monks from the major world religions to exchange ideas. "Monasticism is a bridge between religions," wrote William Skudlarek, OSB, chair of the Monastic Inter-religious dialogue in his review of my book titled *Alone in Community: Journeys to Monastic Life Around the World*. His statement echoes Merton's belief.

Much of Father Louis's life story is familiar to me from books written by him and by others. Ironically, he himself hungered for solitude but relished socializing with colleagues and friends. His first published book, *Seven Storey Mountain*, was released in 1948, the year of my birth. According to the documentary, the book sold ten thousand copies its first day on the shelves and more than a half million copies in its first year. Who would have guessed that the autobiography of a Trappist monk would become a best-seller?

The narrator shares Merton's comments about the book: "Life is not so simple as it once looked in *Seven Storey Mountain*. Unfortunately, the book was a best-seller and has become a kind of edifying legend or something. That is a dreadful fate." I nod in agreement, pleased to know that he felt the way he did. "It is a youthful book, too simple, too crude. I'm doing my best to live it down. I rebel against it and maintain my basic human right not to be turned into a Catholic myth for children in parochial schools."

The film presents the man as a complex spiritual being rather than a whitewashed religious figure sanitized by the Church censors. The more objective look at the monk makes it easier for me to relate to him. The narrator notes that Merton was immoderate as a youth. He drank alcohol, smoked cigarettes, and partied to excess. While a student at England's Cambridge University he fathered a child for whom he never took responsibility. That particular event was cause for his guardian to demand that he return to the United States; both of Merton's parents had died by the time he was fifteen. Shortly thereafter, he enrolled in New York's Columbia University, and a few years later, he was baptized into the Roman Catholic Church.

"What a revelation it was to discover so many ordinary people in one place together more conscious of God than of one another." The narrator reads aloud Thomas Merton's description of his Manhattan parish. "Not there to show-off their clothes but to pray or at least fulfill a religious obligation not a human one." Not long after his baptism, Merton entered Kentucky's Abbey of Gethsemani as a postulant.

Merton joined the monastery in the 1940s, a time when Trappists were living a more physically demanding medieval lifestyle that began each morning at 2 a.m. Their diet was strictly vegan, and they slept, fully clothed, on straw-filled mattresses in unheated dormitories. Each man was limited to writing four letters a year. The life was an "utter detachment from worldly pleasures," explains the narrator. There were no choices; everything was planned. That aspect of the life probably appealed greatly to Merton. At least in the beginning of his monastic life, Merton was desperate to find a disciplined and organized daily schedule. For his first eight years at the monastery he was cloistered.

To my surprise, the man whom I saw earlier in the sanctuary walks quietly into the video room without saying a word. I stop the tape, motion for him to join me in the nearby chair, and push "play" once he is settled in. I am thoroughly engrossed in this exposé of a monk whom I have admired for years.

The documentary recounts Merton's life in the 1960s, when he became an outspoken writer on the issues of civil rights, the Vietnam War, and the unchecked growth of the military-industrial complex. "It is my intention to make my entire life a rejection, a protest against the crimes and injustices of war and political tyranny," stated Merton as he sought to extend his role and influence beyond the monastery walls.

Nicaraguan Renaissance man Ernesto Cardenal also appears in the film. I had the privilege of meeting and talking with him when I traveled to Nicaragua in 1985. The white-bearded, beret-wearing Cardenal greatly admired the Trappist monk. He explains that Merton imparted to him the message that "monks couldn't consider themselves contemplatives unless they also committed themselves to every aspect of the community, its political, its social, its economic life—everything."

Merton's statements of conscience enraged conservative Church leaders and many political and military pundits in the United States. They wanted the Trappist to stick to the topics of prayer and contemplation, but he was determined to advocate living Christian values in the "real" world. Merton's commentaries on issues then facing U.S. citizens are even more pertinent today.

"With the race troubles of the south one can see the beginnings of a Nazi mentality in the United States," he said not long after the 1963 church bombing in Birmingham, Alabama, that left four children dead. "There is a powerful and influential alliance of business and military men who consider everyone who disagrees with them a Communist, a traitor and a spy. The atmosphere is not unlike what I remember from Germany of 1932." Merton could easily have been talking about our current state of affairs.

By the end of the film I am reenergized, fired up, and I want to talk about Merton. I am hoping that my fellow viewer will be interested. As the video rewinds, I introduce myself and share a few things about my background. He says his name is John, and tells me that he lives in Milwaukee. John has never heard of Thomas Merton and, to my disappointment, doesn't seem interested in discussing the documentary. But he clearly wants to talk.

"I'm unemployed right now," he reveals. "I'm a welder and trying to pick up odd jobs, but I'm not having a lot of luck." Over six feet tall, he has a full head of curly brown hair, a bushy moustache, and a slight paunch. His face is scarred and rough but handsome.

"What brought you here?" I ask.

"I came with my friend, Norbert," John explains, his tall frame draping over the metal folding chair. "We have been friends since we were kids." He stretches both legs out in front of him, crosses one over the other, and then folds his arms over his chest. "Norbert's very much into saying the rosary and doing it all the right way."

To my surprise, John tells me that he used to be a member of the Hare Krishna movement, a Hindu religious sect. It is hard to imagine this giant of a man wrapped in a dhoti, his head shaved except for a narrow ponytail, striding down a city street in sandals passing out Hare Krishna literature. It is even harder to visualize the welder dancing ecstatically on a street corner while chanting their mantra "Hare Krishna, Hare Krishna, Krishna Krishna, Hare Hare, Hare Rama, Hare Rama, Rama Rama, Hare Hare" to the hypnotic beat of hand drums. For the Hindu sect, Krishna and Rama are deities, incarnations of the highest form of the Supreme One. In chanting the mantra, members are praising God.

"I went to New York with the Hare Krishna and worked there for a time," he says. "Later I was sent to Japan and India." The Indian pilgrimage city of Vrindaban is their international headquarters. "Then I was sent with a female companion to begin work in Seoul, South Korea." He pauses for a minute, perhaps wondering whether he wants to continue with the story. "Well, let's just say it wasn't a good match and we split up. And I ended up coming back to Milwaukee." His unconventional spiritual journey fascinates me. I respect his willingness to make such a leap of faith.

John says that he still has the utmost respect for Hare Krishna devotees and continues to believe much of what they profess. "In fact, I still travel to Chicago every once in a while to visit their temple and share a meal with them."

I, too, used to visit a Hare Krishna temple when I lived in Washington, D.C. Once a week they would invite the outside community to share in a vegetarian meal, and I would go and participate in religious conversations with the community. I appreciated their company and respected their religious path. They lived collectively and led a disciplined spiritual existence. The one thing that all religious traditions have in common is the "transfer of human consciousness through spiritual discipline," says Merton in the documentary that we just finished watching.

It is clear that the welder wants to continue our conversation, but I have lost my second wind. I am ready for bed and begin to walk toward the staircase.

"Are you going to Vigils in the morning?" he inquires.

"I don't plan on it," I reply. "Probably see you at breakfast. Good night."

Likenesses of Harry Potter's archenemies, the Dementors, pursue me in my dreams. The gigantic black, faceless threesome chases me into dark alleys and abandoned buildings and down an endless one-lane blacktop. The deadly trio repeatedly surrounds me and sucks the air right out of my lungs, leaving me gasping for breath. When they temporarily disappear, I get up and start running again, but they reappear, and the pursuit begins anew.

Tossing restlessly, I awake repeatedly, gasping for air, but each time I fall back into the dream. Finally, I turn on the table lamp, prop myself up in bed, and begin reading a collection of poetry written by a Sufi master that I brought with me.

Brother Felix, the official guest master, tracks me down at breakfast and relays some unexpected news. "There has been a mix-up of retreat dates," the monk cordially informs me. "We have you scheduled for last week rather than this week." Somehow, I must have switched the dates around. I apologize. Felix says that this weekend is filled with reservations. "You will need to vacate your room in the morning." I had planned to spend the entire weekend and leave on Monday before noon. Although I am disappointed, I am hopeful that even a brief stay will provide the insight that I am seeking.

After finishing a second cup of coffee, I wander down to the gift shop, and meet Father Pius. "This monastery was established in the mid-1800s," he informs me with a hint of an Irish accent. "At one time there were 150 active monks. Now there are less than a third of that number." Pius says that he came to the United States from Ireland more than sixty years ago. After taking his final vows at Mount Melleray Abbey in County Waterford, Ireland, the mother house to New Melleray Abbey, Pius volunteered to join the community in Iowa. "I'm eighty-five years old," reveals the tall, white-haired man with hunched shoulders and large hands. As we talk, he casually passes me a pen and the shop guest register and motions for me to sign it.

Father Pius is responsible for shop sales and maintaining the stock. The cluttered room, a contrast to the well-organized spaces I have seen elsewhere in the complex, is a random collection of icons, rosaries, and crosses interspersed among books, cassette tapes, and compact disks. There are also personal cards and food gifts from other Trappist communities around the country. In particular, I notice boxes of sweets made by the Trappistine community located nearby.

Gregarious and welcoming, the senior monk says that he will gladly share some monastic history with me. Pius doesn't expect much activity in the shop until the retreat groups arrive tomorrow. "Old monks are wild as well as simple," wrote Peter Levi in *The Frontiers of Paradise: A Study of Monks and*

Monasteries. "They perch more lightly on the globe than the rest of us" (p. 15).

Pius tells me that farming is the community's primary source of income on their 3,400 acres. "We used to raise beef and dairy cattle as well as pigs and sheep and chickens," he says. "But in the 1970s we began making a transition to crop farming." Today they grow alfalfa and corn, soybeans and potatoes, and also oats. Pius mentions that there are also fruit orchards on the property. Proudly, he informs me that New Melleray also has the second largest privately owned forest of hardwoods and softwoods in the state of Iowa.

Something that Father Pius doesn't mention, but I discover months later when reading *Sanctuaries: A Guide to Lodgings in Monasteries, Abbeys, and Retreats*, is the community's commitment to organic farming. The book's authors, Jack and Marcia Kelly, write that 250 acres have been set aside for certified organic crops. "We commit ourselves to sustainable agriculture that will protect the ecological health of our environment and provide for the economic and social well-being of our community," states the monks' vision statement. "We realize our land provides sustenance not only for ourselves but for the generations who will succeed us" (p. 84). Good stewards of the land, these monks provide a role model for neighboring farmers and the rest of the country.

I leave the old monk to his paperwork and walk outside for some fresh air, but I am again confronted with an overcast sky and frigid winds that sting my face. In the immediate vicinity there is not much to break the force of the wind. I step carefully; everything in sight is coated with ice. This geography is so unlike Assumption Abbey, hidden away and protected on all sides by the dense woodlands. Here the gently rolling landscape exposes the monastic complex to the elements.

Back inside the guest quarters, I climb the stairs to the second floor, retrieve my copy of Frank Bianco's *Voices of Silence*, and wander down to the guest library. Although I have read the book twice, I keep returning to a passage that refers to an experience that the author had when writing about the Kentucky Trappists. It occurred when he and his wife were visiting friends for dinner.

At the dining room table Bianco was asked to describe his project. And when he did, one of the other guests became noticeably upset with his explanation. "Who wants to know about people who have dropped out, who have shrugged off all responsibility to our own society, so they could run away and indulge their insecurity?" the guest commented tersely. I have heard similar reactions when talking of my monastic experiences. Such comments demonstrate ignorance of the monastic life.

"Thomas Merton, like other monks, generally responded [to such questions] by asking why monks were obliged to justify their career decision," writes Bianco. After all, monasteries are self-supporting communities that offer a refuge to the spiritually starved outsider and provide an alternative role model for living together in spirit and community.

Frank Bianco has more to say on the issue. "He [Merton] doubted whether modern society could understand even if an answer were attempted." Bianco points out how difficult it is in a materialistic culture, where the primary goals in business are profit and pleasure, to accept the well-being of the community over the individual. "Westerners (and Americans in particular) find it incomprehensible that any mature adult would willingly submit to regimentation that they perceive as designed to erase individual identity." He cites the example of a Trappist monk choosing a new name when he enters the community. "Like French foreign legionnaires, who also take an assumed name when they enlist, the Trappist's former identity ceases to have any consequence" (p. 28).

While spending time in the library I also come across a booklet titled "New Mellerary Abbey." No author is noted. Inside is a germane quotation that highlights Bianco's point about the erasure of identity: "Renouncing the need for special recognition and exaggerated accomplishment, the monk acquires freedom of self-forgetfulness as he learns to serve others with the talents God has given him." The last page of the booklet mentions New Melleray's Latin motto, *Vacate et videte* ("Be empty and see").

At the noon meal, I choose again to eat at the table designated for silence, a practice at many of the larger monasteries that I have visited. A "silent" table is a welcome respite to some on retreat. While eating I recall with appreciation the dining room camaraderie at the Assumption Abbey, experienced less than a month ago. And yet, silent meals feel appropriate in this community where many of the Ozark monks took their final vows, at a time when more than a hundred men were living here.

"Large communities tend to be more formal and structured," writes M. Basil Pennington in *Monastery*. "They tend to possess more and have more to care for, for they must support more people. In a smaller community, life can be more immediate, simple and poor. A larger community offers greater freedom than a small community where everyone must be present almost all the time to keep things going." Pennington completes his thought: "In a large community monks can take turns, dividing up chores and providing back-up services for each other. If some, or even many, are absent life goes on" (p. 71). His remarks bring to mind the tight schedules lived by the Assumption Abbey monks, where each man has seemingly endless responsibilities.

Returning to the gift shop after lunch, I discover Father Pius once again "perched lightly" over the small counter completing more paperwork. When I enter he immediately puts it aside, pulls up a chair, and makes me feel welcome. "Before I became a monk my name was Mike Hanley," he reveals. Sounds like a strong Irish name, I tell him, and he nods in agreement. "At the time, the superior [the abbot] at Mount Melleray Abbey in Ireland had some connection to Pope Pius and suggested that I replace the name Mike with Pius. So I did." The octogenarian is a fountain of information. He informs me that there are almost a hundred Trappist monasteries in the world and lists many of the forty countries in which they are located. "The largest number is still in France where the order was founded."

Knowing that I have made several retreats at Assumption Abbey, Pius shares something of interest about that community. He says that they were seriously considering closing the monastery after the sale of their concrete-block factory because they didn't have an alternative way to make money. "But that wasn't God's plan," declares Pius. "A monk from our Massachusetts monastery convinced the Missourians to produce fruitcakes, and 'the rest is history.'"

Before leaving him to his paperwork, I ask Pius if after eighty-seven years of life he has a single bit of advice. He doesn't hesitate giving it. "Be willing to say you're wrong when the other person is right," says the Irishman. "Just say, 'Okay. You are right and I am not.'"

Sunday morning Mass is uncommonly crowded. Squeezed between two other worshippers in the pew immediately behind the railing, I sit preoccupied with my own thoughts. There is something intensely desirable about losing myself in a large sanctuary designed for worship. As Peter Matthiessen comments in *Circle of Life*, "To this day, I am drawn joyfully to cathedrals in every land—mosques and temples, too—the stone, the light, the soaring naves, the murmuring and mystery and quiet. With gratitude, I kneel and lose myself amidst the bent humanity crouched in the pews. In the great hush, we breathe as one" (Cohen, p. 228). A monk moving quickly down the aisle toward the visitors' section catches my eye and redirects my attention to the service. He stops abruptly at the railing, opens the gates, and invites us into the greater sanctuary to celebrate the Eucharist.

The officiating priest is the New Melleray abbot. He was visiting Assumption Abbey, along with the Trappistine abbess, the night I arrived there. I feel as though I have come full circle. This brief stay in Iowa is both the beginning and the end of my monastic journey. "Through Him, with Him, and in Him, in the unity of the Holy Spirit, all glory and honor is yours . . . ," we repeat with the abbot as the brilliant winter sunlight streams down upon us from the arched windows above.

A young woman wearing jeans and a college sweatshirt sits alone eating breakfast at the silent table after Mass. Her light blond hair is pulled back tightly into a long ponytail. When I approach the table, she greets me with a smile and a nod—an invitation into the silence. "Many people ask me to speak," writes Henri Nouwen in *The Genesee Diary*. "But nobody as yet invited me for silence" (p. 134). I accept her invitation and sit down next to her. When I finally get up to leave, we simply shake hands.

Near the dining room exit sits Milwaukee John in an animated conversation with Father Pius. Stopping at their table, I place my hands together in front of my chest and bow slightly. "Hare Krishna," I greet the two men.

The welder promptly stands up, places his hands in front of his chest, bows slightly and responds, "Hare Rama."

Leaning over the confused-looking Father Pius, I embrace the senior Irishman, thank him for his hospitality, back away, and walk out the door.

~

Afterword

I have returned to Assumption Abbey several times in the years since my extended retreat. During those brief visits—none more than a few days—I have become aware of some changes in the community. And, more recently, Father Mark has informed me of others.

Since the conclusion of Father Cyprian's term as abbot, three men have served in that capacity: one man was elected to a six-year term, another served briefly as a temporary superior, and the current abbot, Father Mark, was elected for a six-year term. Mark, a man in his early forties, was formerly a member of the Trappist Abbey of New Clairvaux in California.

There have been many construction projects in the community. To meet the continued demand for their fruitcakes, the monks constructed a fully equipped bakery building and hired three people from the outside community to help them with the business. "Our fruitcake industry has grown increasingly and is doing very well," says Abbot Mark. "The product is excellent, rightly esteemed, and the work involved is perfect for a small and aging community."

The abbey has also added a new infirmary and private quarters for the monks, a new classroom and office space, and an exterior cloister and garth (enclosed garden). Also, the monks' refectory and chapter room where the monks meet weekly to discuss community issues have been renovated.

There has been some deconstruction at Assumption Abbey as well. The old monastery, affectionately referred to as the Swiss chalet, has been torn down. And the railing in the sanctuary separating the visitors' section from the monks' has been removed.

But the community is much more than buildings, and there have been changes in other areas, too. Father Theodore, the abbey's capable, dedicated, longtime business manager, has passed away. The energetic and good-spirited guest master, Father Richard, has slowed down considerably due to a series of illnesses. And my furry four-legged antagonist, Dyers, has died.

Rather than a guest master, the abbey now has a guest mistress. A gregarious and jovial Irish American laywoman was hired to fill the job. She is a delightful addition to the guest wing.

One of the community hermits, Father Robert, has moved from his old "tar-paper shack" into a new dwelling, which he has named the Bark Avenue Hermitage. "It has all the conveniences to make life easier—hot and cold water, shower and a bathroom," according to Robert. "Even has a telephone now but no radio, TV, computer, or newspapers." He adds, "So now I need to be careful not to be 'stifled by comfortability.'" Other than those changes, Father Robert reports that his life remains the same.

The small community has also gained members. Abbot Mark informs me that three new members have joined the community. All of them have changed their stability to Assumption Abbey. One man arrived from the Trappist monastery in California, and another came from Assumption Abbey's daughter house in the Philippines. "The third new monk is a transfer from a Benedictine monastery," says Mark. He is "discerning his vocation to the eremitical life." So in the near future, there may be three hermit monks living on the Assumption Abbey grounds.

"In addition, several men have come for longer or shorter periods of time to try the life," according to the abbot. "At present we have one novice, forty-two years old." Two monks from the daughter house are just completing a two-year stay in Missouri. Soon they will return to their native country.

Unchanged, and unchanging, at Assumption Abbey is the daily rhythm of the monks' lives: the timeless rituals of prayer, *lectio divina*, and daily manual labor; all necessary to nourish the life of the community and the spiritual growth of each monk. The brothers maintain their unwavering commitment to hospitality; however, because of increased demand for personal retreats, interested individuals are encouraged to make reservations months in advance.

Bibliography

Benedict, St. *The Rule*. New York: Cooper Square, 1966.

Bianco, Frank. *Voices of Silence: Lives of the Trappists Today*. New York: Paragon House, 1991.

Bly, Robert, James Hillman, and Michael Meade, eds. *The Rag and Bone Shop of the Heart: Poems for Men*. New York: HarperCollins, 1992.

Brueggeman, Walter. *Hopeful Imagination: Prophetic Voices in Exile*. Philadelphia: Fortress Press, 1986.

Camus, Albert. *The Myth of Sisyphus*. New York: Penguin Books, 1942.

Capps, Walter. *The Monastic Impulse*. New York: Crossroads, 1983.

Cardenal, Ernesto. *To Live Is to Love*. Translated by Kurt Reinhardt. New York: Herder & Herder, 1972.

Chittister, Joan. *Wisdom Distilled from the Daily: Living the Rule of St. Benedict Today*. San Francisco: Harper & Row, 1990.

Claassen, William. *Alone in Community: Journeys into Monastic Life Around the World*. Leavenworth, Kans.: Forest of Peace, 2000.

Cohen, David, ed. *The Circle of Life: Rituals from the Human Family Album*. San Francisco: Harper, 1991.

Directory of Intentional Communities: Guide to Cooperative Living. Evansville, Ind.: Community Publication Cooperative, 1990.

Heat-Moon, William Least. *Blue Highways: A Journey into America*. Boston: Little Brown, 1982.

Holman, Nancy, and Robert D. Beckett. "Faith and Fruitcakes: Peace, Solitude, and a Tasty Treat at Assumption Abbey." *Rural Missourian*, December, 1992.

Holyhead, Verna A. *The Gift of St. Benedict*. Notre Dame, Ind.: Ave Maria Press, 2002.

Johnson, Fenton. *Keeping Faith: A Skeptic's Journey*. Boston: Houghton Mifflin, 2003.

Jones, W. Paul. *The Province beyond the River: The Diary of a Protestant at a Trappist Monastery*. Nashville, Tenn.: Upper Room, 1981.

———. *Teaching the Dead Bird to Sing: Living the Hermit Life Without and Within*. Brewster, Mass.: Paraclete Press, 2002.

Kelleher, Ray. "Kathleen Norris," *Poets & Writers Magazine*, May/June, vol. 25, 1997.

Kelly, Jack, and Marcia Kelly. *Sanctuaries: A Guide to Lodgings in Monasteries, Abbeys, and Retreats of the United States*. New York: Bell Tower, 1991.

Kierkegaard, Søren. *Journals and Papers*, vol. 1. Bloomington: Indiana University Press, 1967.

Kingsolver, Barbara. *The Poisonwood Bible*. New York: HarperCollins, 1998.

Kramer, Dewey Weiss. *Open to the Spirit: A History of the Monastery of the Holy Spirit*. (Conyers, Ga.: Monastery of the Holy Spirit, 1986).

Leahy, Donna, comp. *Wisdom of the Plain Folk: Songs and Prayers from the Amish and Mennonites*. New York: Penguin Studio, 1997.

Lernoux, Penny. *Cry of the People: United States Involvement in the Rise of Fascism, Torture, and Murder and the Persecution of the Catholic Church in Latin America*. Garden City, N.Y.: Doubleday, 1980.

———. *People of God: The Struggle for World Catholicism*. New York: Viking, 1989.

Levi, Peter. *The Frontiers of Paradise: A Study of Monks and Monasteries*. New York: Weidenfeld & Nicolson, 1987.

Merton, Thomas. *The Asian Journal of Thomas Merton*, edited from his original notebooks by Naomi Burton, Patrick Hart, and James Laughlin. New York: New Directions, 1975.

———. *The Seven Storey Mountain*. New York: Harcourt, Brace, 1998.

Mowat, Farley. *Never Cry Wolf*. Boston: Little Brown, 1963.

Norris, Kathleen. *The Cloister Walk*. New York: Riverhead Books, 1996.

Nouwen, Henri J. M. *The Genesee Diary: Report from a Trappist Monastery*. Garden City, N.Y.: Doubleday, 1976.

Osmin, Collin, and Peter Turner, eds. *Creative Camera International Yearbook*. London: Coo Press Ltd., 1976.

Partridge, Elizabeth. *Restless Spirit: The Life and Work of Dorothea Lange*. New York: Viking, 1998.

Pennington, M. Basil. *Monastery: Prayer, Work, Community*. New York: Harper & Row, 1990.

Pirsig, Robert. *Zen and the Art of Motorcycle Maintenance*. New York: Morrow, 1974.

Rise Up Singing: The Group Singing Songbook. Bethlehem, Pa.: Sing Out Corp., 1988.

Roberts, Elizabeth, and Elias Amidon, eds. *Life Prayers from Around the World: 365 Prayers, Blessings, and Affirmations to Celebrate the Human Journey*. New York: HarperCollins, 1996.

Samuels, Sam Hooper. "A Quiet Weekend with the Monks." *New York Times*, February 18, 2005.

Saroyan, William. *The Time of Your Life*. New York: Harcourt Brace & Co., 1939.

Smith, Robert Lawrence. *A Quaker Book of Wisdom: Life Lessons in Simplicity, Service, and Common Sense*. New York: Eagle Brook, 1998.

Songs of the Spirit. Burnsville, N.C.: World Around Songs, 1978.

Sullivan, Maureen. *101 Questions and Answers on Vatican II*. Mahwah, N.J.: Paulist Press, 2002.

Teilhard de Chardin, Pierre. *The Divine Milieu: An Essay on the Interior Life*. New York: Harper, 1960.

Thoreau, Henry David. *Walden*. Princeton, NJ: Princeton University Press, 1971.

Weil, Simone. *Waiting for God*. New York: Harper & Row, 1973.

Wilkes, Paul (director/producer), and Audrey L. Glynn (producer). *Merton: A Film Biography*. New York: First Run Features, 1984.

~

About the Author

William Claassen is a longtime social activist, writer, traveler, photographer, and teacher. His broad range of interests, from politics and cultural diversity to comparative religions and the arts, have taken him to forty countries on five continents. Claassen's previous book, *Alone in Community: Journeys into Monastic Life Around the World*, is a personal exploration of monastic traditions in all of the major world religions. He lives in Oakland, California.